George Copway

Indian life and Indian history

George Copway

Indian life and Indian history

ISBN/EAN: 9783337305116

Printed in Europe, USA, Canada, Australia, Japan

Cover: Foto ©Andreas Hilbeck / pixelio.de

More available books at **www.hansebooks.com**

AND

INDIAN HISTORY,

BY AN INDIAN AUTHOR.

EMBRACING THE

TRADITIONS OF THE NORTH AMERICAN INDIANS REGARDING
THEMSELVES, PARTICULARLY OF THAT MOST
IMPORTANT OF ALL THE TRIBES,

THE OJIBWAYS.

BY THE CELEBRATED KAH-GE-GA-GAH-BOWH,
Chief of the Ojibway Nation;

KNOWN ALSO BY THE ENGLISH NAME OF

GEORGE COPWAY.

BOSTON:
ALBERT COLBY AND COMPANY,
20 Washington Street.
1860.

TO AMOS LAWRENCE, ESQ.,

Of Boston, Mass.

THIS VOLUME,

WITH FEELINGS OF DEEP GRATITUDE,

AND SENTIMENTS OF THE HIGHEST RESPECT,

IS AFFECTIONATELY INSCRIBED

BY

KAH-GE-GA GAH-BOWH.

CONTENTS.

PREFACE.

In compliance with the oft-repeated request of a number of literary friends I present this volume to the public. In doing so there is another motive that has influenced me, and I may be pardoned, if here, at the commencement of my task, I briefly record it.

In thus giving a sketch of my nation's history, describing its home, its country and its peculiarities and in narrating its traditionary legends I may awaken in the American heart a deeper feeling for the race of redmen and induce the pale-face to use greater effort to effect an improvement in their social and political relations.

You must know that my advantages have not been very great for the attainment of knowledge ; that, in common with my forest brethren I have, as the saying is, " been brought up in the woods." I feel incompetent for my work, but, am impelled forward by the though that the nation whose history I here feebly sketch seems passing away and that unless a work like this is sent forth, much, very much that is interesting and instructive in that nations actions will with it pass away.

Though I cannot wield the pen of a *Macaulay* or the graceful wand of an *Irving* with which to delineate an Indian's life, yet I move a pen guided by an intimate knowledge of the subject it traces out, the joys and the sorrows it records.

It is not many years since I laid aside my bow and arrows, and the love for the wild forest, born with me, I yet retain. Twenty months passed in a school in Illinois has been the sum-total of my schooling, save that I have received in the wide world. During my residence of six years among the pale-faces I have acquired a knowledge of men and things, much, very much more I have yet to learn, and it is my desire that my brethren in the far west may share with me my crust of information; for this end I have labored and do labor, and will continue to labor, till success crowns my efforts or my voice and hand are silent in the home of the departed.

To the Christian and the Philanthropist, I present

in these pages an account of the rise and progress of events which have greatly advanced the moral eleva-tion of my nation. Should they see in it anything to stimulate them to greater action, now is the time, the hour to act. It can be proved that the introduction of Christianity into the Indian tribes has been produc-tive of immense good. It has changed customs as old as any on the earth. It has dethroned error, and has enthroned truth. This fact is enough to convince any one of the unjustness and falsity of the common say-ing, that, " the Indian will be Indian still."

Education and Christianity are to the Indian what wings are to the eagle that soar above his home. They elevate him ; and these given to him by men of right views of existence enable him to rise above the soil of degradation and hover about the high mounts of wisdom and truth.

To the man of letters I would say, that in compli-ance with your request I am aware how far short I have fallen from satisfying you with a recital of the Ojibways' history.

Much has been lost to the world, through a neglect of educating the red-men who have lived and died in the midst of educationary privileges but have not been allowed to enjoy them. They hold a key which will

1*

unlock a library of information, the like of which is
not. It is for the present generation to say, whether
the last remnants of a powerful people shall perish
through neglect and as they depart bear with them
that key.

Give the Indian the means of education and he will
avail himself of them. Keep them from him and let
me tell you he is not the only loser.

The Indians at present mingle with the whites.
The intercourse they have had together has not in all
instances elevated the character of the former. The
many hundreds of rude careless, fearless whites who
have taken up their abode in frontier regions have induced the red-men to associate and unite with them
in practices of dissipation. To the Americans at home
I look for an antidote for this evil, which they as well
as myself must most sincerely regret.

Friends, Christians, your love for mankind extends
beyond the border. Your love for mankind has penetrated the forests, and is to-day shedding its holy influence on many a happy group assembled around a
birchen fire. May you not tire or grow faint.

The history of the Ojibways like that of other Indian tribes is treasured up in traditionary lore. It has
been passed down from age to age on the tide of song,

for there is much poetry in the narrative of the old sage as he dispenses his facts and fancies to the listening group that throng around him.

As the first volume of Indian history written by an Indian, with a hope that it may in some degree benefit his nation, and be the means of awakening an interest for the red-men of America in those whose homes are where they once lived and loved, this work is sent forth tremblingly, yet with hope by its Author.

KAH-GE-GA-GAH-BOWH.

AN INDIAN VILLAGE.

CHAPTER I.

THE extent of territory occupied by the Ojibway nation, is the largest of any Indian possessions of which there is any definite knowledge.

When the Champlain traders met them in 1610, its eastern boundary was marked by the waters of Lakes Huron and Michigan. The mountain ridge, lying between Lake Superior and the frozen Bay, was its northern barrier. On the west, a forest, beyond which an almost boundless prairie. On the south, a valley, by Lake Superior, thence to the southern part of Michigan. The land within these boundaries has always been known as the country of the Ojibways. It comprises some of the most romantic and beautiful scenery. There are crystal waters flowing over rocky beds, reflecting the mighty trees that for centuries have reared their stout branches above them. There are dense forests which no man has entered, which have never waked an echo to the woodman's axe, or

.

sounded with the sharp report of a sportsman's rifle. Here are miles of wild flowers whose sweet fragrance, is borne on every southern breeze, and which form a carpet of colors as bright and beautiful as the rainbow that arches Niagara.

The woodland is composed of a great variety of trees, mostly pine, hemlock, oak, cedar, and maple. As the traveller approaches the north, he will meet birch tamarach, spruce, and evergreen.

In going from east to west, along the borders of the lakes, the scenery is so changing and of such kaleidescope variety and beauty that description is impossible. There is room and opportunity for adventure among the bold, broken, rugged rocks, piled up one upon another in "charming confusion," on the shores, along the borders of the silent waters, or beneath the solid cliffs against which the waters of Superior break with a force which has polished their rocky surface.

The mountains, rivers, lakes, cliffs, and caverns of the Ojibway country, impress one with the thought that Nature has there built a home for Nature's children.

THEIR LAKES.

IT is unnecessary for me to describe minutely every lake that exists in the Ojibway territory. I will mention those of greatest note, and which the traveller as

he stood upon the shore has viewed with an admiration
bordering on idolatry; for, surely, were there anything
besides the Creator worthy of worship it would be His
works.

At one time the easternmost lake of the Ojibways
was Huron. But they have, by their prowess, gained
the waters of Ontario and Erie.

Lake Huron is of great depth. Its waters are known
by their beautiful clearness, and by the fact of their
rise and fall once in every seven years. Its shores
were lined with their canoes at a period shortly subsequent to the introduction of fire arms into their midst.
Rock abounds in great quantities, and the wood con-
sists mainly of cedar, hemlock, pine, and tamarach.
The hills rising in the south and in the north-east,
present to the observer a very imposing appearance.

From the main there juts forth a point of land, on
one side of which is Georgian Bay or Owen's Sound
and the lake. The ledge of rocks near this has the
appearance, at a distance, of a fortification. When the
waters are calm and clear these rocks can be seen in
huge fragments beneath their surface as if thrown
there by some giant in other days.

The great depth of the water of this lake has induced the belief among the Indians that it has a connection with other lakes, and possibly with the sea,
and it has been supposed that such is the cause of its
rise and fall once in a certain number of years.

Many stories are told of monsters who are said to inhabit these waters and of the cause of the flowing of the water in the channel of the Manettoo Islands on the coast.

As before stated the water of this lake is very clear. In the year 1834 while journeying upon its northern borders I dropped a small silver coin. It rapidly descended till it was lodged upon a rock. I could see it very distinctly. I attached a cord to an axe and lowered it till it touched the rock on which the money lay. On drawing it up and measuring the length of the cord I found, to my surprise, that the coin which I could see so distinctly was at a distance of seventy three feet from the surface of the water and about seventy five or eighty feet from where I stood.

The bays near this lake are the Pantonogoshene, (Falling-Sand Bay,) and the Thunder Bay. The islands are numerous, and a three days' journey among them would convince any one that they are numbered by thousands. They are very similar to those in the St. Lawrence, known as "the thousand islands," masses of rock, as if thrown up by some mighty convulsion of nature. Many, however, are covered with low cedars, imparting to them a somewhat lovely and attractive appearance.

The north-west and easterly winds cause an ebb and flow of water in the lake. The wind passes to one side of the chain of islands, which runs in a line parallel with the north shore. It then rushes to and from the other extremity of these islands, and thus causing a continual current. But other causes than this, effect the rise and fall, on return of seven years. These have been differently defined by different individuals. The cause assigned by H. R. Schoolcraft, Esq., has been most generally received as the true one. I am not prepared to state here in full my own reasons for this singular fact, but I am in hopes to give them before long.

On the shores of Huron have been fought some of the most severe battles between the Chippewas and the Iroquois. French River, Saganaw Bay, and Sagueeng, have been the scenes of these bloody and disastrous conflicts.

Lake Superior, or, as it is named in the Ojibway language, *Ke-che-gumme*, is situated in the centre of the nation, and is not only the largest of its lakes, but the largest lake of water in the world. It has been called the "Great Lake of the Ojibways."

This is the most remarkable of all lakes, not merely on account of its size, but on account of the picturesque scenery around it, and the almost innumerable traditions related of it and its borders. Every point of land, every bay of water has its legendary story to tell, and it is this that renders Lake Superior superior to all others in point of interest. This lake extends about five hundred miles from east to west;

the distance around is about fourteen hundred miles. The immense body of water within these limits are at times calm and placid; at others, furious and foaming, and as the waves lash the shores, the thunder of their voice echoes and re-echoes amid the rocky caverns which their constant action has made.

From the highlands of "Grand Cape" or "Frog Hills" can be obtained one of the grandest views to be had on the lakes. Twenty-three miles from these are the celebrated "Falls of St. Mary's." Many, whose love of adventure has surmounted their fear of danger, have gone up in canoes above these falls, and from the summit of these hills have been doubly paid for their journey by the wide-extended view of the broad lake spread out before them.

The sandy beach extends from "White Fish Point" southerly towards the Pictured Rocks, a distance of upwards of one hundred and fifty miles. At the upper end of this beach are the Sand Hills rising abruptly from the waters edge to a height of over three hundred feet. Next to these in point of interest are seen "the Pictured Rocks" which extend fourteen miles beyond the sandy beach.

All of the southern shore presents a bold and rugged appearance; and the northern is for the most part of the same character.

The towering cliffs that border the lake, appear like giant sentinels; particularly at night, when the bright

light of the rising moon causes them to cast their sha-
dows, do they thus appear, standing in bold relief with
trees upon their sides, whose waving branches seem
to give life to the tall-guards.

These heights are connected with many traditionary
stories; and, according to the superstition of our forefathers, the heroes of many romances loiter upon their
sides.

Red Lake, Leach Lake, Mill Lake and Lake Win-
nipeg are in the North.

Leach Lake is noted as being the resort of wild
fowl. They are there found in great numbers, being
attracted to the spot by the wild rice which is there
met with in vast quantities.

The waters of Mill Lake flow into the Mississippi
River. It is about sixty miles in circumference. · Its
shores abound with valuable cornelian stones, and its
adjacent woods with a great variety of game.

THEIR RIVERS.

THEIR Rivers are the largest in the world. First in
importance and magnitude is the Mississippi, on whose
banks for two thousand miles can be seen the most
enchanting scenery. The St. Lawrence flowing from
the source of the St. Louis River, at the head of Lake
Superior, from lake to lake, till the vast body precipi-
tates itself over the Falls of Niagara, and sweeping by

B

"the Thousand Islands" and over the Lachiene Rapids, mingles with that of the Gulf of St Lawrence. Another stream flows from near the head of the Mississippi. Red River flows from the edge of the Prairie, first westward, but soon changes its course, and passes in a northerly direction till the frozen regions stay its farther progress.

These mentioned, are the principal rivers from which they drank in that happy time when they knew not of that insidious foe,—"the fire water."

In addition to these there are a number of rivers, which, in any other country would be considered "great." Those flowing into the Mississippi are the Crow-wing, St. Croix, Chippeway, and Wisconsin. Those flowing into the St. Lawrence are the Montreal and Burnt-wood. I speak of those in the Ojibway country. Near Huron are the Mohawk, Sagianaw, Tranti, and others running their waters into the Lakes.

When I look upon the land of the Ojibways I cannot but be convinced of the fact that in no other portion of the world can there be a territory more favored by Heaven. The waters are abundant and good; the air bracing and healthy; and the soil admiringly adapted for agricultural purposes. It is not much to be wondered at that in such a climate, such a strong, athletic and hardy race of men should exist, as the Ojibways are generally acknowledged to be. In fact, they could scarcely be otherwise. There is as much difference between them and many tribes of the South as there is between the strong wind and gentle zephyr.

THEIR MOUNTIANS.

THE mountains are few. There are, however, quite a number of eminences, not exactly to be rated under the name of mountains and I am sure cannot be called level earth. There are many heights along the southern shore of Lake Superior and some in the north to which the title of mountains is applied. There are numerous lofty peaks of granite, a short distance back from the shore of Lake Huron and the northern shore of Lake Ontario. I have walked over that part of the country for many days in succession and have seen nothing but these granite hills, most of which are destitute of wood. There was a time when they were well covered with trees that took root in the clefts, but they were all destroyed by fire and the peaks to-day present a very barren and inattractive appearance.

The Porcupine Mountains near La Point, can be seen, in a clear day, at a distance of eighty miles from their base. One of the grandest sights I have ever witnessed, was a view of this range of mountains, at a distance, when the morning sun was rising above their summits, and a fog from the lake enveloped their tops. It was indeed worth the night's journey to behold.

The Missawbay Heights are formed of ledges of rock, piled one upon another, and lie in a line parallel with the north-west shore. There are numerous mountains and hills on the northern shore of Lake Superior. The elevation known as "the Thunder Mountains," have the singular appearance of a lion crouching for its prey. A curious legend is told of this range, which will be related in a subsequent chapter.

The Caraboo Heights, below the Thunder Mountains, are deserving of mention. They are viewed with admiration by all tourists who approach them. Upon these heights are to be seen figures, claiming the attention of those curious in ancient lore, which, if rightly interpreted, might possibly furnish a clue to the origin of the Chippeways.

There is another mountain, the only one in fact, that is visible from the lake at a great distance. Adjacent to the mountains are numerous hills, thickly wooded and carpeted with rich moss, soft as velvet and of beautiful variegated colors.

The mountainous edge, near the source of Lake Superior on one side, and the Mississippi River on the other, is quite high. It commences on the south shore of Lake Superior, and runs in a westerly direction, to the head of the river St. Croix.

I have now given an imperfect outline of the lakes,

rivers, and mountains of the country occupied by the Ojibways. It is in the midst of such that they now and have for years lived. There they roamed to the chase and hastened to the field of combat. Their canoes floated by the shores of those mighty lakes, or glided smoothly down the stream. On those waters they departed at early dawn, and returned at dusk with loads of venison.

The war-cry resounded among those cliffs and rocky passes, and the merry shout and song of children gladdened the old chieftain's heart.

In 1610, from each of those thousand islands the smoke arose from the wigwams of a numerous tribe.

That was the day of their glory and prosperity. Then their shouts of triumph were answered from peak to peak, for a distance of two thousand miles west, and four hundred north.

Review what has been said. Look at their country and say has any nation possessed a better. The mountains of the north covered with evergreens, shading the wide lakes. The high hills on the south, rising cliff upon cliff, till the uppermost is concealed by the clouds. The Missaw Bay Heights on the west, standing like towers in naked grandeur, looking down with contempt, as it were, on the hundred streams whose roar rises with the mist which envelops their summits.

Deep ravines, through which the streams as they pass sing the songs of nature in soft strains, till gathering strength, the waters dash over rocks in deep caverns, and thunder forth in heavier tones.

I have stood on one of the mountain peaks and seen a column of snow descending upon the icy waters of Lake Superior, a distance of fifty miles, and it has taken one day and a-half to reach the edge of the lake which lay at the base of the mountain.

The sun rises and sets with beautiful effect. Its rays resting upon the clouds and reflected from them, clothe the whole extent in robes of fire ; every hill seems blazing with the glory of the sun. In every ray is seen the spirit of poetry.

Suppose yourself standing at a distance, and behold ing one of the nation going up the mountain's side near him the waters of Superior—

" Lay weary and still after storm."

Over his head the forest trees waved their heavy branches. Behold him ! he stands there ruler of the forest world. One of Nature's sons standing in her own battlements. His erect and manly form, his easy, graceful motion, are true indications of the exalted soul that lives its active life within. Living as he does, amid the happiest creations of the Great Creator, he cannot but adore and worship Him. His devotion is pure. He

" Sees God in storms and hears Him in the wind."

Nature points him up to Nature's God. I love my
country; and will any of my readers condemn a child
of the forest for loving his country and his nation?

"Land of the forest and the rock—
  Of dark-blue lake and mighty river—
Of mountains reared aloft to mock
The storm's career, the lightning's shock—
My own green land forever!"

I cannot better close this chapter than by subjoining
the following graphic description of " The Pictured
Rocks," given by General Lewis Cass:

" Upon the southern coast of Lake Superior, about
fifty miles from the Falls of St. Mary, are immense,
precipitous cliffs, called by the voyageur Le Fottrail,
the Pictured Rocks. This name has been given them
in consequence of the different appearances which they
present to the traveler, as he passes their base in his
canoe. It requires little aid from the imagination to
discern in them the castellated tower and lofty dome,
and every sublime, grotesque, or fantastic shape, which
the genins of architecture ever invented. These cliffs
are an unbroken mass of rocks, rising to the elevation
of three hundred feet above the level of the lake, and
stretching along the coast for fifteen miles.

" The voyagers never pass this coast except in the
most profound calm; and the Indians, before they
make the attempt, offer their accustomed oblation, to

propitiate the favor of their Monitas. The eye instantly
searches along the eternal rampart, for a single place
of security; but the search is vain. With an impas-
sable barrier of rocks on one side, and an interminable
expanse of water on the other, a sudden storm upon
the lake would as inevitably assure destruction of the
passenger in his frail canoe, as if he were on the brink
of the cataract of Niagara.

" The rock itself is a sand-stone, which is disinte-
grated by the continual action of the water with com-
parative facility. There are no broken masses upon
which the eye can rest and find relief. The lake is so
deep, that these masses, as they are torn from the
precipice, are concealed beneath its waters until it is
reduced to sand. The action of the waves has removed
every projecting point.

" When we passed this immense fabric of nature,
the wind was still and the lake was calm. But even
the slightest motion of the waves, which in the most
profound calm agitates these eternal seas, swept
through the deep caverns with the noise of the distant
thunder, and died away upon the ear, as it rolled
forward in the dark recesses inaccessible to human
observation.

" No sound more melancholy or more awful ever
vibrated upon human nerves. It has left an impres-
sion which neither time nor distance can ever efface.

" Resting in a frail bark canoe, upon the limpid

waters of the lake, we seemed almost suspended in the
air, so pellucid is the element upon which we floated.
In gazing upon the towering battlements which im-
pended over us, and from which the smallest fragments
would have destroyed us, we felt, and felt intensely
our own insignificance.   No situation can be imagined
more appalling to the courage, or more humbling to
the pride of man.   We appeared like a small speck
upon the broad face of creation.

"Our whole party, Indians, voyagers, soldiers, officers, and servants, contemplated in mute astonishment
the awful display of creative power, at whose base we
hung ; and no sound broke upon the ear to interrupt
the careless roaring of the waters.   No cathedral, no
temple built with human hands, no pomp of worship
could ever impress the spectator with such humility,
and so strong a conviction of the immense distance
between him and the Almighty Architect."

CHAPTER II.

In listening to the traditions of the Indians in their wigwams, the traveller will learn that the chiefs are the repositories of the history of their ancestors. With these traditions there are rules to follow by which to determine whether they are true or false. By these rules I have been governed in my researches.

The first is to inquire particularly into the leading points of every tradition narrated.

The second is to notice whether the traditions are approved by the oldest chiefs and wise men. Such are most likely to be true, and if places or persons are mentioned, additional clue is given to their origin and proof obtained of their truth or falsity.

The chiefs have generally been those who have at all times retained a general history of their nation.

From the year 1831, to the present time, I have

been in communication with our nation, with every portion of it. All appear to adopt the belief that most of the Indians came from the west. The present Ojibways, or those now called Messamgans, settled in Canada West after the years 1634 and '35. They came over from St. Marie's River to Lake Huron, and relate in their traditions an account of those who came to the Falls of St. Marie from *Pe-quab-qua-wav-ming*, near the Avee Bay, on the south shore of Lake Superior. Others, no doubt, in the year 1642, came to this northern shore of the lake. I have heard that these came from La Point, or *Shah-gah-wab-nick*. In this place the Indians lived a long time. Still they trace their own trail to the waters of Red and Sandy Lakes, which places they all, or nearly all, look back to as the home of their forefathers. War came, and in their exercise of it against other nations, they moved eastward from La Point and towards the south against the *Sioux*.

When they moved from Red and Sandy Lakes, it was the fisheries of Lake Superior that attracted them from their old haunts and induced them to leave the scenes to which, for so many years, they had been accustomed.

The same attraction is supposed to have drawn the Sioux to the south-west end of Lake Superior and to the land bordering all along below *Sha-gah-wab-nick*. In a short time contentions arose between the Ojibways and the Sioux about the right of occupancy. The game of the land and the fish of the waters was probably the first cause of hostility between the two powerful nations,—a hostility which has been marked by many acts of cruelty on both sides. War commenced for the retention of the hunting-lands, and a neutral ground having been between them ever since, the first cause of other wars has been forgotten, and the repeated ravages of death made upon each party have obliterated the remembrance of the cause of the early contention.

DISTRIBUTION OF LAND.

I HAVE heard a tradition related to the effect that a general council was once held at some point above the Falls of St. Anthony, and that when the Ojibways came to this general council they wore a peculiar shoe or moccasin, which was gathered on the top from the tip of the toe, and at the ancle. No other Indians wore this style of foot-gear, and it was on account of this peculiarity that they were called *Ojibway*, the signification of which, is *gathering*.

At this council the land was distributed. That part which fell to the lot of the Ojibways is said to have been the surrounding country of Red Lake, and afterwards Sandy and Leach Lakes, which statement coincides with that of the chiefs of the village of La Point, or the Shah-gah-wah-mick.

The Sauks were once a part of the Chippeway family, as also were the Menomenies and the Ottawas. About the year 1613 the latter began to leave the main body near Lake Superior. When the traders of Champlain began their operations with the Chippeways, the French called them " the trading Indians," (Ottawas.) The Sauks fought with the Sioux on the upper waters of those lakes which run down from the southern shores of Lake Superior. They also engaged in combat with the Shawnees of southern Illinois.

Though the Ojibways occupied but a small piece of territory at first, they soon extended their dominions to the very borders of the snow-clad hills of the north, and in the streams of that cold region watched for the beaver, whose furs were wrought by them into warm clothing.

It was at a date just prior to Pontiac's time, that the Ojibways met the Shawnees on the waters of Erie and united with them in a successful war against the Iroquois in Canada West, after which the two, Ojibways and Shawnees, settled down in the country of the Hurons.

The battle-grounds are yet to be seen, and many marks of the savage warfare are now visible.

1634 and 1635 were years of glorious triumph. The nation had sought intercourse with the French in Montreal, and their communication was carried on by journeys through the lands of an intermediate nation.

The intercession resulted in a long and disastrous war, in which the Ojibways were victorious. After this they enjoyed a free communication with the French, with whom they have had friendly intercourse from that time to the present.

They fought their way through the lands of hostile nations from the west end of Lake Superior along the entire lake country. The shores of Lake Superior, Lake Huron, and the River St. Lawrence, abound with their battle fields. The dust of many a brave now lies there, friend and foe in one common resting-place.

Exciting stories of the doings of those days have been passed down from mouth to mouth. So the old man related them the blood of the young Ojibways ran swiftly through his veins, and his eye shone with the fire of enthusiasm.

The war-whoop's shrill notes have now died away. Now the wigwam stands undisturbed, and the hymn of peace is chanted within their thatched walls.

Behold the change! Commerce urged on by the pale-face, strides rapidly and withlessly into their midst, and orders them back, back, back, to make way for its houses and its merchandize. Scarce is he camped, ere once again he is told to go farther west. When will the last order be given? When will the red-man have a home?

INDIANS HUNTING A BEAR.

CHAPTER III.

THEIR WILD GAME.

THERE is, doubtless, a greater variety of game to be found in the Ojibway Country than in any other equal extent of Western territory. The northern part is not so well supplied with large game as that district near the head waters of the Wisconsin, Chippeway, St. Croix, Mississippi and Red Rivers.

Small game is to be found on the Northern shores of the Lakes with the hardy Reindeer, such as the Rabbit, Lynx, Martin, and Fisher. The three latter have been a source of much profit on account of their furs. The rabbit has been the principal game for the Northern Indians, who snare them for their food and skins. These latter are made into strings and woven into blankets.— They also make their garments of these skins, and are dressed in them from head to foot. The eyes of a pale face would considerably extend on beholding a fellow

3

in such accoutrement. These Indians reside in the interior of the shores of Lake Superior, in the North. We
call them (Nopeming Tah-she-e-ne-neh) *Backwoodmen.*
The deer are found in almost all parts of the country,
though not as much in the North as in the South. In
the spring they migrate to the North, and return to the
South in the fall, few ever wintering in the North on
account of the great depth of snow in that quarter.

This animal was killed in four different ways before
the introduction of fire-arms. The first was by a snare
formed of a rope of wild hemp, and so placed that when
the deer's neck was caught, the more stir he made the
more he could'nt stir. At every movement the cord
would wind about the neck tighter and tighter, until he
was choked, for at one end of the rope would be fixed a
small rail, which the large end slips off, and in falling
it prys upon the deer, who in a short time dies. When
they wished to get through soon, they placed these
snares all around for half a day, then drive the deer all
over the snares until some are caught.

The second was by driving sharp spikes of wood into
the ground on the deer path, just the other side of a log
over which they would be expected to jump. In jumping the logs, they must fall upon these sharp spikes,
which would pierce them through, and thus kill them.

The third way was to drive the deer with dogs into the water, when, being out of their element, they could be captured. In winter, instead of driving them into water, a short chase in the deep snow would soon tire them, and they were soon at the disposal of the hunter.

The fourth and last manner of killing them was by means of bow and arrow. Bows were made of a power to enable them to shoot through the side of a deer without any difficulty. The Indian watched at the " Salt Licks," or at the borders of lakes or rivers, to which the deer often go to feed on the grass. An Indian can shoot a deer in the woods at a distance of fifty paces.

The bow was generally made of iron-wood or red cedar; sometimes of hickory, well seasoned. The arrows were made like spikes at the end. Before they had iron, they used bone and shell for the ends : the shells were carved in such a manner as to admit of being pointed at the end of the arrow. I have no recollection of killing but one deer with an arrow, as fire arms came into the field of action as soon as I did. I remember being at the foot of Rice Lake, Canada West, with others on a hunting tour in the night. Soon after nine o'clock, we heard the animal feeding in the grass by the shore. Having a lighted candle, we placed it in a three-sided lantern ; opening one side, the light was

C

thrown upon the deer only. By this contrivance we were enabled to approach so near it in our canoe, that it appeared to be but ten or fifteen paces from us. I drew my bow-string—the arrow winged its way—the deer made a few short leaps, and died.

During my travels in the East, I have met with individuals whom I found it difficult to convince that the Indian's arrow could execute so much, and doubted me when I told them that with it they killed deer, bears, and such like.

Several years ago, in the State of New-York, an elderly gentleman, a farmer and myself were entertained by a kind family to tea. The gentleman monopolized all the time for conversation with questions about the Indian mode of life. I answered them all as well as I could, though some of them were so *very* odd, that it was with the exercise of the greatest muscular strength that I could refrain from laughing in the inquisitive person's face. He seemed satisfied with all my answers except those in relation to killing deer with bow and arrow.— He doubted. He could'nt bring his mind to believe such a thing possible. After laboring half an hour to convince him of the fact that we could, he turned aside, firmly resolved not to believe me. I held my tongue, half mad ; and made the proposition that the next day

I would make a bow and a couple of arrows, and as I understood he was a farmer, I should get him to furnish a yearling calf, and if in shooting I did not hit it, I would pay him the price of the calf if he desired it ; but if, on the contrary, I should hit it, and kill it, then it should be mine ! While our friends at the table could not wait till the morrow to know the result, my friend, the doubting gentleman, coolly declined, saying he *believed* we could kill deer at sixty paces if we hit it at all. I and my friends endeavored to provoke him to accept my proposition, but failed to accomplish our purpose, his avarice overcoming his unbounded curiosity !

Bears are also taken by means of bow and arrow.— They are very easily captured in winter, for then they are found in hollow logs and in the ground enjoying their winter quarters. The black bear is to be found all over the Ojibway country. They are more numerous in years when fruit and acorns are abundant. Some of the Ojibway people believe the bear to be a transformed being ; in other words, that it was once a more intelligent creation, and for this reason they profess a great veneration for its head and paws, but not so much for *its meat,* for they relish that very highly, and seem to forget its former intelligence when indulging their appetites with a savory steak. The head and paws are festooned with colored cloth and ribbons, and suspended at the upper end of the Indian's lodge. At the nose they bestow a very liberal quantity of tobacco, as a sort of peace-offering to the dead animal.

In early life I received a lecture from my father upon hunting. He related many cunning stories of the bear, and I remember I got so courageous that the next day I was all the time in a perfect fright, thinking every brush heap I met the hiding place of some old Bruin.

In the year 1832, I made my first appearance as a bear hunter. It was in the fall of the year that I with others left our homes with the intention of being absent for three or four weeks. We went down Crook's Rapids below Rice Lake, to hunt. I remember how skittish I felt at first, as I shouldered my gun and followed the six hunters before me into the woods, for just then all the cunning stories I had heard were fresh in my mind. We came to a halt about three miles distant from our starting place, and the head hunter, my father, gave his companions a brief description of the face of the country and of the places to which the bear would be most likely to resort, for then they were eating acorns. Around us we could see newly-made tracks of the deer and bear; my lips parched, and my whole body fevered with anxiety. When my father had finished his account, he

turned to me, and said :—" My son, don't go very far ;
keep behind the rest as you hear the firing of guns, and
when you think it is time to return, you can come round
this way and go towards home :" then, waving his
hand, off the party started in every direction. I, too,
went one way.

When I lost sight of the others of my party, all the
" cunning stories" about the bear—of its hiding under
rotten logs, of its pretending to die, and its sudden attacks, rushed upon my mind. I was soon roused from
my reverie, for in less than twenty minutes I heard the
reports of guns from all directions ; but for all this I
walked along as well as I could, looking out for a bear
which I was *afraid of seeing*, and yet *hunting for*.

I would walk along in the open space, so that I might
see my bear at a distance, and not come suddenly upon
him or he upon me. The guns were fired every few
minutes. I could see, occasionally, deer at a distance
running at full speed. While I was passing along at
the foot of the hills on which the thick foliage concealed
the logs, which lay piled one upon another, I heard a
tremendous crash near the top. I stood, as if transfixed
to the spot, and sure enough, I could see the branches
of the young trees waving, and thought I could see objects approaching me. I scarce dare to wink, and trem-

bled in my scarlet leggins, when to my dread astonishment I saw a large bear coming down towards me, like
a hogshead rolling down a hill! I jumped behind a
pine tree, and prepared for the combat. He came at me
at a full gallop, and I feared the worst. When he had
approached to within five paces from me, I thought it
time to define my position, and make some demonstra-
tion of war. I sprang from my hiding place, and alighted
upon the ground. I hallooed at the top of my voice,
" Yah !" and at the same time pointed the muzzle of my
gun to the white spot on the breast of the animal. I
fired, and the smoke enveloped myself and the bear.—
As I did so, I fell to the ground, and a bundle of leaves
which the bear had scratched up in his " exercises" fell
upon my face. This I thought to be the bear, and falling backward, I expected the fellow would get to be
quite loving of his new-found companion, and in the
transports of his joy, hug me to death. But when I
raised my head, I learned my mistake, and beheld a
tremendous animal apparently in the agonies of departing life. I arose, picked up my gun, which had fallen
from my hand, and immediately reloaded it, in order to
be prepared if his actions proved to be a farce instead of
a tragedy. I took a long pole and poked him considerably. He did not show any signs of life. Yet so doubt-

ful was I of his death, that I left him. Thus ended my first adventure on a bear-hunting excursion.

In the immediate vicinity of Lake Superior, Indians trap bears in large " dead falls." Near Red and Lead Lakes, they take them when crossing the water. Some years ago, they were thus captured at the head of Lake Superior.

The Moose and Deer are also taken, chiefly however in the Northern parts of Lake Superior and in the vicinity of Red Lake. The Moose is one of the largest animals found, and the hunters have quite a merry time when three or four are taken at one time. It is considered best to take them before they leave their yard in the winter. If they are not thus taken, it is very difficult to secure them, as they are very fleet.

The Reindeer is taken in all parts of the North West. It is the hardiest animal in the country. They are often chased for days in succession by the Indians, and a coat of ice is seen to cover them, caused by their perspiration ; at the same time a thick steam arises from them. They go in droves, and when they are on the run, the light snow rises in clouds in every direction.— The skin of the deer, as well as the skins of all the animals I have mentioned, are manufactured into clothing, and are oftentimes dressed in a beautiful manner and highly ornamented.

The Elk is to be found in the West, on the neutral
ground lying between the Sioux and Ojibway nations ;
at the head waters of the Wisconsin ; in the Northern
parts of Michigan, and near the Chippeway, St. Croix,
Rum and Red Rivers.   This is one of the noblest looking animals in our country.   When on the run its head
is held high, its back curved, on which its large horns
appear to rest.   At one time, in 1837, I saw a drove of
five hundred ; and a more animating sight I never beheld.   I shot one, and being at that time a prisoner at
the foot of Lake Pepin, and wishing to be generous to
my enemies, I took it to the chief of the tribe that held
me.   Soon after I was liberated, and with my cousin
Johnson was permitted to depart.

The Buffalo is taken only at the head of Red River,
where the Chippeways and the half-breeds kill between
eight and ten thousand every year.   The Indians form
into companies and take their wagons with them when
they go on a Buffalo hunt.   The drove of Buffalo is
very large, and grazing they blacken the prairie as far
as the eye can reach.

The tread of the Buffalo makes the earth to tremble.
The hunters are mounted on ponys, who are so taught
that when a wounded animal falls they immediately
start for an encounter with another.   The Indian gath-

ers his arrows from the grass while he is riding at
full speed—a feat which is considered very dexterous, but which is quite common on the western prairies.

Before leaving this noble animal, I must indulge my
readers with what a recent writer says respecting it :
prefacing it with the remark that the Bison and the
Buffalo are one and the same.

" From the species of the ox kind the Bison is well
distinguished by the following peculiarities. A long
shaggy hair, clothes the fore parts of the body, forming
a well marked beard, beneath the lower jaw, and descending behind the knee in a taft; this hair rises on
the top of the head in a dense mass nearly as high as
the extremities of the horns. Over the forehead it is
closely curled and matted so thickly as to deaden the
power of a rifle ball, which either rebounds or lodges in
the hair, merely causing the animal to shake his head
as he heavily bounds along. The head of the Bison is
large and ponderous, compared to the size of the body :
so that the muscles for its support, necessarily of great
size, give great thickness to the neck, and by their origin
from the prolonged dorsal vertebræ processes, form
the peculiar projection called the hump. This hump is
of an oblong form, diminishing in height as it recedes,

so as to give considerable obliquity to the line of the neck.

The eye of the Bison is small, black and brilliant; the horns are black, and very thick near the head, where they curve upwards and outwards, rapidly tapering towards their points.

The outward line of the face is convexly curved, and the upper lip, on each side being papillons within, dilates and extends downwards, giving a very oblique appearance to the lateral gap of the mouth, in this particular resembling the ancient architectural bas-relief, representing the heads of oxen. The physiognomy of the Bison is menacing and ferocious, and no one can see this animal in his native wilds without feeling inclined to attend to his personal safety.

The summer coat of the Bison differs from his winter dress rather by difference of length than by any other particulars.

In summer from the shoulders backward, the hinder parts of the animal are all covered with a very fine short hair that is as smooth and soft to the touch as velvet.

The tail is quite short and tufted at the end, and its utility as a fly brush is very limited. The color of the hair is uniformly dun ; but the long hair on the anterior parts of the body is, to a certain extent, tinged with yel-lowish or rust color. These animals, however, present so little variety in regard to color, that the natives con-sider any remarkable difference from the common ap-pearance as resulting from the immediate interference of the Great Spirit.

Some varieties of color have been observed, though the instances are rare.

A Missouri trader informed the members of Long's exploring party, that he had seen a greyish white Bison, and a yearling calf, that was distinguished by several white spots on the side, a star or blaze in the forehead, and white fore-feet. Mr. I. Doughty, an interpreter to the expedition, saw in an Indian hut a very well pre-pared Bison's head with a star on the front. This was highly prized by the proprietor, who called it his great medicine; for, said he, the herds come every season to the vicinity to seek their white companion.

In appearance, the Bison cow bears the same relation to the bull as is borne by the domestic cow to her mate. Her size is much smaller, and she has much less hair on the fore-part of her body. The horns of the cow are much less than those of the bull, nor are they so much connected by the hair.

The cow is by no means destitute of beard ; but

though she possesses the conspicuous appendage, it is quite short when compared with that of her companion.

From July to the latter part of December the Bison cow continues fat.

Their breeding season commences towards the latter part of July, and continues until the beginning of September, and often the cows separate from the bulls in distinct herds, and bring forth their calves in April.

The calves rarely separate from the mother before they are a year old, and cows are often seen accompanied by calves of three seasons.

The flesh of the Bison is somewhat coarser in its fibres than that of the domestic ox, yet travellers are unanimous in considering it equally savory as an article of food; we must however receive the opinions of travellers on this subject with allowance for their peculiar situation, being frequently at a distance from all other food, and having their relish improved by the best of recommendations in favor of the present viands,— hunger.

It is with reason, however, that the flesh is said to be more agreeable, or the grass on which these animals feed is short, firm and nutritious, being very different from the luxurious and less saline grass produced on a more fertile soil.

The fat of the Bison is said to be far sweeter and richer, and generally preferable to that of the common ox.   •

The observations made in relation to the Bison's flesh when compared to the flesh of the domestic ox, may be extended to almost all wild meat, which has a peculiar flavor and raciness, which renders it decidedly more agreeable than that of tame animals, although much coarser, and the fibre by no means so delicate.

Of all the parts of the Bison that are eaten, the hump is most famed for its peculiar richness and delicacy, because when cooked 'tis said very much to resemble marrow.

The tongue and marrow bones are also highly esteemed by the hunters."

Before dismissing the subject of game, I must mention those animals that are taken principally for their fur. I cannot enter into a detailed account of these. The furs brought into the market by the Ojibways, have ever been considered the best. They consist for the most part of Beaver, Otter, Martin, Fisher and Lynx.

The interior of the Canadian country, between the shores of Ontario, Huron and Lake Superior, was once well hunted for the beaver, but its pelt being here valueless, they are increasing in numbers.

These are some of the animals caught by the Ojibways on land. There is an abundance of fish in all their waters. The best of these is the sweet fish of the lakes, *Sis-ka-way*, which is esteemed a very great delicacy; and many others which I will not mention, lest I should weary my readers, but will allow them to swim from my sight.

CHAPTER IV.

" Fantastic, frolicksome and wild,
With all the trinkets of a child "
COTTON.

I believe all the Indian nations of this Continent have amusements among them. Those of the Prairie nations are different from those of the Ojibways, suitable to their wide, open fields. The plays I am about to describe are the principal games practised by the people of my nation. There are others ; and chance games are considerably in vogue among them.

One of the most popular games is that of ball-playing, which oftentimes engages an entire village. Parties are formed of from ten to several hundred. Before they commence, those who are to take a part in the play must provide each his share of staking, or things which are set apart ; and one leader for each party.

4

Each leader then appoints one of each company to be stake-holder.

Each man and each woman (women sometimes engage in the sport) is armed with a stick, one end of which bends somewhat like a small hoop, about four inches in circumference, to which is attached a net work of raw-hide, two inches deep, just large enough to admit the ball which is to be used on the occasion.— Two poles are driven in the ground at a distance of four hundred paces from each other, which serves as goals for the two parties.   It is the endeavor of each to take the ball to his hole.   The party which carries the ball and strikes its pole wins the game.

The warriors, very scantily attired, young and brave fantastically painted—and women, decorated with feathers, assemble around their commanders, who are generally men swift on the race.   They are to take the ball either by running with it or throwing it in the air. As the ball falls in the crowd the excitement begins.— The clubs swing and roll from side to side, the players run and shout, fall upon and tread upon each other, and in the struggle some get rather rough treatment.

When the ball is thrown some distance on each side, the party standing near instantly pick it up, and run at full speed with three or four after him at full speed.—

The others send their shouts of encouragement to their own party. "Ha! ha! yah!" "A-ne-gook!" and these shouts are heard even from the distant lodges, for children and all are deeply interested in the exciting scene. The spoils are not all on which their interest is fixed, but is directed to the falling and rolling of the crowds over and under each other. The loud and merry shouts of the spectators, who crowd the doors of the wigwams, go forth in one continued peal, and testify to their happy state of feeling.

The players are clothed in fur. They receive blows whose marks are plainly visible after the scuffle. The hands and feet are unincumbered, and they exercise them to the extent of their power; and with such dexterity do they strike the ball that it is sent out of sight. Another strikes it on its descent, and for ten minutes at a time the play is so adroitly managed that the ball does not touch the ground.

No one is heard to complain, though he be bruised severely, or his nose come in close communion with a club. If the last mentioned catastrophe befell him, he is up in a trice, and sends his laugh forth as loud as the rest, though it be floated at first on a tide of blood.

It is very seldom, if ever, that one is seen to be angry because he has been hurt. If he should get so, they

D

would call him a "coward," which proves a sufficient check to many evils which might result from many seemingly intended injuries.

While I was in La Point, Lake Superior, in the summer of 1836, when the interior band of Chippeways, with those of Sandy Lake, Lac Counterville, Lac De Frambou, encamped in the Island, the interior bands proposed to play against the Lake Indians. As it would be thought a cowardly act to refuse, the Lake Indians were ready at an early hour the next day, when about two hundred and fifty of the best and swiftest feet assembled on a level green, opposite the mansion house of the Rev. Mr. Hall.

On our side was a thicket of thorns ; on the other the lake shore, with a sandy beach of half a mile. Every kind of business was suspended, not only by the Indians, but by the whites of all classes.

There were but two rivals in this group of players. One of these was a small man from Cedar Lake, on the Chippeway river, whose name was *"Nai-nah-aun-gaib,"* (adjusted feathers,) who admitted no rival in bravery, daring, or adventure, making the contest more interesting.

The name of the other competitor was *" Mah-koonce,"* (young bear,) of the shore bands.

The first, as I said before, was a small man. His body was a model for sculpture; well proportioned. His hands and feet tapered with all the grace and delicacy of a lady's. His long black hair flowed carelessly upon his shoulders. On the top of his raven locks waved in profusion seventeen signals (with their pointed fingers) of the feathers of that rare bird, the western Eagle, being the number of the enemy he had taken with his own hand. A Roman nose with a classic lip, which wore at all times a pleasing smile. Such was *Nai-nah-aun-gaib*. That day he had not the appearance of having used paint of any kind. Before and after the play I counted five bullet marks around his breast.— Three had passed through; two were yet in his body. Besides these, there were innumerable marks of small-shot upon his shoulders, and the graze of a bullet on his temple.

His rival on this occasion was a tall muscular man. His person was formed with perfect symmetry. He walked with ease and grace. On his arms were bracelets composed of the claws of grizzly bears. He had been in the field of battle but five times; yet on his head were three signals of trophies.

The parties passed to the field; a beautiful green, as even as a floor. Here they exhibited all the agility and graceful motions. The one was as stately as the proud Elk of the plains; while the other possessed all the gracefulness of the Antelope of the western mountains.

Shout after shout arose from each party, and from the crowds of spectators. "Yah-hah—yah-hah," were all the words that could be distinguished. After a short contest the Antelope struck the post, and at that moment the applause was absolutely deafening. Thus ended the first day of the play, which was continued for some length of time.

After this day's game was over, the two champions met and indulged in a sort of personal encounter with the ball. This they continued a short time, then parted company, in good humor, and mingled with the crowd.

The Moccasin play is simple, and can be played by two or three. Three moccasins are used for the purpose of hiding the bullets which are employed in the game. So deeply interesting does this play sometimes become, that an Indian will stake first his gun; next his steel-traps; then his implements of war; then his clothing; and lastly, his tobacco and pipe, leaving him, as we say, "*Nah-bah-wan-yah-ze-yaid;*" a piece of cloth with a string around his waist.

The " Tossing Play" is a game seldom seen among the whites. It is played in the wigwam. There is used in it an oblong knot, made of cedar boughs, of length, say about seven inches. On the top is fastened a string, about fifteen inches long, by which the knot is swung. On the other end of this string is another stick, two and a half inches long, and sharply pointed. This is held in the hand, and if the player can hit the large stick every time it falls on the sharp one he wins.

" Bone Play," is another in-door amusement, so called, because the articles used are made of the hoof-joint bones of the deer. The ends are hollowed out, and from three to ten are strung together. In playing it they use the same kind of sharp stick, the end of which is thrown into the bones.

Doubtless the most interesting of all games is the " Maiden's Ball Play," in the Ojibway language, *Pah-pah-se Kah-way.*

The majority of those who take part in this play are young damsels, though married women are not excluded. The ball is made of two deer skin bags, each about five inches long and one in diameter. These are so fastened together as to be at a distance of seven inches each from the other. It is thrown with a stick five feet long.

This play is practiced in summer beneath the shade

of wide-spreading trees, beneath which each strives to
find their homes, *tuhwin*, and to run home with it. These
having been appointed in the morning, the young women
of the village decorate themselves for the day by painting their cheeks with vermillion, (how civilized, eh ?)
and disrobe themselves of as much unnecessary clothing
as possible, braiding their hair with colored feathers,
which hang profusely down to the feet.

At the set time the whole village assemble, and the
young men, whose loved ones are seen in the crowd,
twist and turn to send sly glances to them, and receive
their bright smiles in return.

The same confusion exists as in the game of ball
played by the men.   Crowds rush to a given point as
the ball is sent flying through the air.   None stop to
narrate the accidents that befal them, though they tum-
ble about to their no little discomfiture ; they rise making a loud noise, something between a laugh and a cry,
some limping behind the others, as the women shout.
" *Ain goo*" is heard sounding like the notes of a dove, of
which it is no bad imitation.   Worked garters, moccasins, leggins and vermillion are generally the articles at
stake.   Sometimes the Chief of the village sends a par-
cel before they commence, the contents of which are to
be distributed among the maidens when the play is over

I remember that some winters before the teachers from
the pale faces came to the lodge of my father, my mother was very sick. Many thought she would not re-
cover her health. At this critical juncture, she told my
father that it was her wish to see the " Maiden's Ball
Play," and gave as a reason for her request that were
she to see the girls at play, it would so enliven her
spirits with the reminiscences of early days as to tend
to her recovery.

Our family then resided at the upper end of Belmount
Lake, above Crow River. The next day, at early dawn,
the crier of my father was sent around to inform the village damsels that the Ball Game was to be played at
the request of the Chief's wife.

Two large spruce trees were transplanted from the
woods, to holes in the ice ; and in the afternoon the people from the villages were on the shore of the Lake.—
Among them was my mother, wrapt up in furs and
blankets to protect her from the cold. There was just
enough snow upon the ground to make the footing very
uncertain. I scarcely recollect any thing equal to the
sport of that day. The crowds would fall and roll
about, some laughing most heartily at themselves and
at the distorted countenances of their companions, whose
pain could not be concealed. When it was over, they

all stood in a circle, and received the rewards allotted
to each, consisting of beads, ribbons, scarlet cloths, &c.
In a few moments more I heard them in their wigwams
jesting and laughing at their day's sport.

Jumping is an exercise in which my countrymen have
always engaged with considerable interest.   Trials are
made of jumping over a raised stick, or in the sand.—
This sport, as well as the use of the bow and arrow,
young women are prohibited from engaging in.

Foot Racing is much practised, mostly however by
the young people.   Thus in early life they acquire an
elasticity of limb as well as health of body, which are
of priceless value to them in subsequent years.

The first mortification my pride ever received was on
a certain occasion when I engaged in one of these races
in the presence of a crowd of warriors.   The prize was
a piece of scarlet cloth.   As I reached forth my hand
to grasp the prize, a rope that lay hid in the grass upset
me so completely, that I turned half a dozen sommersets
and finally tumbled into a pool of water.   When I got
out I had the extreme pleasure of seeing my rival take
the cloth, and of hearing him brag that he had actually
beaten the Chief's son.   I wiped my drenched head as
best I could, and my eyes of the dirt which adhered to
them with all the tenacity of a leach, amid the shouts

of laughter which was all the consolation I received in my misfortune. Since then I have walked seventy-five miles a day in the spring of the year, so that I can boast of this, if not of my first pedestrian feat.

I need not say in concluding this chapter, what every one probably knows, that the plays and exercises of the Indians have contributed much towards the formation and preservation of that noble, erect, and manly figure for which they are so remarkable.

Growing up in the daily practice of these has been and is now a sure preventive of disease. Not until recently has the rude and brutish system of wrestling been in vogue among them.

The law of the Nation, like that of ancient Greece, has been enacted with a view to the health of its subjects. It obliged the people to engage in these exercises that they might inherit strong constitutions, and be prepared for the cold storms, and the piercing blasts that sweep around the lake shores.

The mildness added to the coldness of the climate conduce to the expansion of the ingenuity of my people. The old saying, " Necessity is the mother of invention," finds a verification in them. Did they possess the advantages of education possessed by the whites, many a bright star would shine forth in their ranks to bless and

improve mankind.   What they want is education.—
They have mind, but it requires culture.

A short time since, while on a steamboat on the waters of the upper Mississippi, a gentleman speaking of
the Chippeways, said that they were a manly, noble
race, that their motto seemed to be, " Suffering before
treachery—death before dishonor."   It was gratifying
to my national pride to hear such an assertion made by
an enlightened American.

CHAPTER V.

" 'Twas blow for blow, disputing inch by inch,
For one would not retreat, nor t'other flinch."

FOR centuries have the Ojibways and Siouxs been at
enmity with each other. Cessation of hostilities for a
few years has only served to strengthen for renewed
conflict. These wars first originated, as I have before
stated, in the question of the right of occupancy of the
fisheries at the upper end of Lake Superior, and the
right to the game of the adjacent woods. Subsequently
they were carried on for conquest, until at length revenge has been the cry of both parties.

The waters of Menesotah have been crimsoned with
the blood of both nations, and the upper Mississippi has
witnessed their unrewarded contest ; and their shouts
and groans have alike resounded among the mountain
passes, and echoed from cliff to cliff on the rock-walled
shore.

The rivers which flow into the Mississippi have floated hundreds of the canoes of the Ojibways, freighted
with resolute warriors against the Siouxs. While the
Siouxs have passed up the same streams, and finding
the smoke of the " *Ah-ah-to-won*" rising from the wigwam, have suddenly startled them with their war-cry.
The heights of Lake Superior have been used as towers
by the Siouxs, from which to watch the sky across the
Lake, while the barrier ridges of the North were used
by the Ojibways for the same purpose. Thus Nature
furnished her children with watch-towers and fortresses.

The quarrels have been kept alive, and the war-fires
fanned by the songs of each nation. As soon as children were old enough to handle a bow and arrow, representations of the enemy were made, and the youngsters
taught to shoot at them, for exercise and practice. The
old men narrated to them deeds of bravery, and thus
were they inspired with a desire to grow up, and when
men, act like their fathers, and scout the wide forests
for each other. Even the mothers have taught their
offspring, before they leave their breast, to hate their
enemies. The Siouxs have, in some instances, acknowledged that our forefathers drove them from the North
West of St. Paul, a lake they call "*E-sab-yah-mah-da*,"
and the upper part of Leach Lake.

Several years ago, while strolling by the Chippeway River, with one of the most intelligent Indian Chiefs, whose name was " Moose Tail," he pointed out to me numerous battle-grounds of days past, and all day sketched to me in his own graphic language the conflicts that had occurred upon them.

I counted twenty-nine battle-grounds on the shores of the Menomence river, along which is a small branch of the Chippeway, on the western side, where trees were notched according to the number of warriors who fell. The border of the St. Croix contains more, and the upper Mississippi can furnish traditional records of battles at every mile of its course.

Above the Falls of St. Anthony, just above the "great bend," one of the deadliest battles was fought; and another near the mouth of the Chippeway.

The Chippeways have gone to war in bands of from two to five, while the Siouxs, in nearly every instance, have had as many hundreds.

Of the recent war, an account of which has been published, on Lake St. Croix and Rum River, it is only necessary to repeat what others have said, that it was brought on by the treachery and cruelty of those in whose power it was to have prevented the sad occurrence. I was on the battle-field of Lake St. Croix soon after the conflict, and saw the remains of the slaughtered Chippeways scattered in all directions. The marks of bullets were upon all the trees, and the shrubvery was all trodden down. Some of the dead were suspended upon the branches of the trees. The Siouxs may have killed a large number of Chippeways, but the warfare was not an honorable one. The day previous, a pipe of peace was received from the Sioux Nation by the Ojibways, who had a desire for peace.

The pipe was expected that day, and was smoked in good faith, but the next day the Siouxs followed the Ojibways up the river, then followed those of St. Croix. The day following they availed themselves of every advantage, and killed over one hundred Chippeways and upwards of ninety Siouxs. Since this conflict, many Americans have settled among them, whose presence has in a great degree prevented a repetition of the same disastrous scenes.

It is by the good influence of the whites· that they will eventually abandon their war life, and betake themselves to the employments of peace. I was glad, during my short stay at Minisota, to see the beneficial results of Gov. Ramsay's efforts among the Indians. They must be induced to give up war and petty strifes before they can be benefitted, morally or physically.

I cannot close this chapter without giving my readers an account of the wars I have referred to. It is written by William Warren, a writer in the " Minisota Pioneer." He has made himself well acquainted with the history of the Ojibways, and is himself by birth, partly, one of the Nation. Writing from Crow Wing River he says :

" A party of one hundred and fifty once laid an ambuscade at the extreme point of *Shaguhwaumik*. The Ojibway lads, crossing over early in the morning to kill ducks, were set upon, but the point being well adapted to defence by numerous sand hills, they fought till the village opposite being alarmed, the warriors began to swarm forth ; and crossing over, landed a mile below the extreme point, cutting the Siouxs entirely off from escape ; all were killed but two, who jumped into the lake, and were never heard of or seen after. The bones of the slain warriors are still visible in particles,throughout the entire point.

The Chippeways tell of a large war party that was raised to march against the then Sioux village of Sandy Lake. The party was so numerous, that the string of warriors reached a great distance as they marched in single file, against the devoted village ; which was taken after a bloody slaughter. This event happened or took place, about one hundred and twenty years ago

The leader's name was *Bauswush*, grand-father of the present Chief of Sandy Lake, now aged about sixty years. The party started from *Fond du Lac.*

Some years after Sandy Lake had been taken by this chief, sixty Ojibway warriors started down the Mississippi on a war party. At the confluence of the Crow Wing and Mississippi rivers, they found on their way back, traces of a large Sioux war party that had gone up, and probably killed their defenceless wives and children. Too late to arrive to their rescue by the signs left, they dug holes on the bank of the river, and laid an ambuscade for their enemies. The Sioux soon came floating down, singing songs of triumph and beating the drum. Their canoes were laden with prisoners, and the scalps of the slain dangled on poles erected in them. The Siouxs numbered three hundred; the party in ambush, but sixty. But when they recognized wives and children as prisoners, and beheld the bleeding scalps of their relatives, the blood boiled in their veins, and, in perfect desperation, they sounded the war-whoop and discharged a flight of arrows on their *triumphant* and confident enemies.

Many canoes were upset, and a few prisoners swam ashore at the first surprise; but the Siouxs rallying, soon effected a landing, and tying their remaining prisoners to trees, a regular Indian fight commenced. When arrows and ammunition had failed, they dug them hiding holes close to one another, and pelted each other with stones. The bravest fought hand to hand with knives and clubs. This fight lasted three days, till at last, the Siouxs retreated, leaving many dead, and most of them prisoners. The Ojibways, satisfied with their revenge, returned to their desolated village.

The marks of this battle and the hiding holes on the bank are still visible, within a few rods from where I am writing.

The Siouxs and Ojibways have met three different times at the confluence of these rivers. The village of Sandy Lake, since the Ojibways have resided there, has twice been nearly depopulated ; once as I have just related, and another time, this band was attacked at Cross Lake, forty miles north of Crow Wing, while in their spring encampment, and all killed and taken prisoners but seven men, four women and three children ; this event occurred about fifty years ago ; and some men are living, who were at that time taken prisoners by the Siouxs, and afterwards returned.

Many battles occurred about Leech Lake and Red Lake of the North. The whole of that region between the Crow Wing and British line, has been conquered

E

from the Siouxs. Many engagements and massacres took place on the St. Croix and Chippeway rivers. Two considerable fights occurred at Elk river, emptying in the Mississippi at a place called to this day by the Indians, 'the battle-ground.'

The marks of these battles are still visible; at the last, was killed a renowned war chief of the Ojibways, who was, in his time, the terror of the Siouxs ; and died much regretted by his tribe. The name of this chief was *Ke-che-waub-e-shash ;* Big Martin. The Ojibways of this district, often speak of him as the one, whose valor and prowess conduced to drive their enemies from the country. Many exploits are told of him, and he died covered with scars received in a hundred fights.

About forty years ago, a party of two hundred warriors under Flat Mouth, Chief of Leech Lake, fell on a camp of Siouxs at Long Prairie, numbering forty lodges; all were killed but six men of the Siouxs. The Ojibways captured many horses, but being unable to manage them, killed them ; and the bones of man and horse are still bleaching on the plain.

About the same time, the *Black Duck*, of Red Lake, was surrounded after destroying a large camp of Siouxs, and he, with forty braves, killed to a man, on the far western plains. He was a renowned warrior and a

brave man. It is unnecessary to mention their different hostile meetings of late years ; for the past ten
years, not less than four hundred Ojibways have been
killed in this war, and we can judge by this, what a
sacrifice of life there has been for the past two centuries.

As many fights, surprises, massacres and single exploits can be told of this endless feud as would fill a
book ; all through the country, from Selkirk's Settlement
to Wisconsin River south, and from Lake Superior to
the Mississippi, spots are shown where the blood of
these two tribes has been freely spilt. Even at this day,
in spite of the white man's interference, it is no strange
thing to hear of surprises and murders on either side,
and to see a warrior with his head stuck full of eagles'
plumes, denoting the number of enemies he has killed
in his time.

One hundred years ago, the Ojibways were hemmed
in along the shores of Lake Superior ; the war path of
their enemies terminated at many of their lake shore
villages. But now they are masters of all the country
to the Mississippi ; and had it not been for the partition
of lands among the Indian tribes, by the United States,
Hole in the day, their late noted war chief, used often
to confidently affirm that he would have made his village at St. Peters, and the hunting grounds of his young

men would have extended far into the western plains of
the Siouxs. All this proves much for their prowess in
war; but they lay the main cause of their success to
their first intercourse with whites; they became possessed of fire arms long before their enemies, and made
good use of them."

The continuation of these wars, up the first of April,
1850, as given by the Minesota Chronicle, is here
related:—

"Our community has just been startled with the intelligence of another of those sanguine scenes so common
in the annals of the two powerful tribes of the Northwest—the Siouxs and the Chippewas. On Wednesday
morning last, about sunrise, a war party of Siouxs from
the village of Little Crow and Red Wing, surprised a
small encampment of Chippewas, on Apple River, Wisconsin, and killed and scalped fourteen of them, without loss or injury to the attacking party. They also
took one boy prisoner. Few men were with the party
of Chippewas—it being mostly composed of women and
children, engaged in making sugar. The fourteen killed comprised three men, three nearly grown boys, six
females, women and children, and two male children.
The attack was upon ground heretofore ceded by the
Siouxs to the Government, but upon which, by treaty

stipulation, they still have the privilege of hunting. The place is 20 or 25 miles north-east of Stillwater.

On Thursday, the Sioux warriors appeared in the streets of Stillwater, and went through the scalp dance, in celebration of their victory—forming a circle round the Chippewa boy—their prisoner—and occasionally striking him on the face with their reeking trophies.— The boy, we understand, has already been adopted into one of the families at Little Crow Village.

It is with pain we record the occurrence of a scene so truly revolting to the better feelings of humanity. This aggression of the Siouxs will doubtless lead to retaliation on the part of the Chippewas ; and we may expect to hear of more bloodshed, unless the civil and military authorities succeed in putting a stop to it. This can hardly be expected with the present meagre force on our frontiers. The murder of the Chippewa on Crow River by the Siouxs a few weeks ago, (who was the son of the Chief White Fisher) had caused much revengeful feeling to break out anew among that tribe, previous to the occurrence we now relate.

It is proper to remark, that the better disposed men among the Siouxs entirely disapprove of this renewal of their old feud against the Chippewas. The leader of the party in this tragedy is a graceless scamp, who last fall scalped his own wife. He was arrested for the act, and confined in the prison at Fort Snelling for several weeks. Having signed the temperance pledge, and promised a reform for the future, he was finally released. It were better had he been kept there till this time. It is said the main reason that induced him to lead his comrades to slay the defenceless Chippewas, was to wipe off the disgrace of his former cruelty to his own family, and the punishment which followed it. Such are the Indian's ideas of honor!

Measures will be taken by Gov. Ramsey to bring the offenders connected with this outrage to justice. The Chippewa boy will be sent back to his people as soon as he can be reclaimed from the Siouxs."

CHAPTER VI.

THE WAR BETWEEN THE IROQUIS AND WESTERN
HURONS, TERMINATING IN THE WARS BETWEEN
THE OJIBWAYS & IROQUIS IN CANADA WEST.

" The death shot hissing from afar,
The shock, the shout, the groan of war."

MORE than two hundred winters have clothed the
mountains of the North with snow, which as many
summer suns have melted, since the battle shout of the
Hurons, in their once happy and peaceful homes, died
away, and the Iroquois shouted their note of triumph.

Long and bloody had been the struggle between the
Hurons and Iroquois when they were heard of by Champlain in the year 1608. The one nation occupied the
whole tract of land about the three lakes Ontario, Erie,
and that which still bears the name of the Nation.

They formed a confederation of five Nations, as did
their brethren the Iroquois, who occupied at that time

the principal part of what is now the State of New-York Few Indian wars have been more sanguinary than those between the Hurons and the Iroquois. The forces on each side were equal, and from childhood they had gradually acquired great expertness in the use of arms, the bow and the arrow : both were innured to climate and fatigue. The whole Huron country was kept in constant commotion, for the Hurons had made depredations upon the Algonquin tribes in the South, North, and West.

When they fell out with their own brethren, the war became a series of sanguinary single combats. The hands of friends become those of enemies, sending forth a declaration of war from the Hurons upon their allies, who had assisted against the Algonquin tribes, and upon whose children they had committed most barbarous acts—acts which could not be forgotten.

The Ottaways, Ojibways and Nenomenees, turned a deaf ear to their cries, and listened not when they came and related their misfortunes. It was heart-rending to see the Huron warrior suppressing his sobs and tears—and many a warrior shouted vengeance on the Hurons with whom they had till then been on peaceable terms. They had not forgotten their former treaties, or that their faith in the sacredness of them, confirmed by the pipe of peace, had been violated. The allies of the Ojibways had been trifled with ; they must now receive the reward of their perfidy, for the frown of that *Monedoo* before whom they had consented to smoke the pipe of peace, rested on them.

The struggle went on—each alternately rent the skies with shouts of victory, which were but momentary.— The wails of the wounded and suffering were heard on the shores of the broad Niagara, and on the banks of the St. Lawrence. The Hurons had penetrated to the North, along the shores of *Mah ah-moo-see-be* (Ottaway river.) Their canoes floated by the banks of the Ontario, Erie and Huron. The inland seas in the northern part of the peninsula were thronged by them. The rivers, mountains, and vallies were all theirs. In such a delightful country were their game and wigwams, and it was for these they fought with a desperation seldom equalled, never excelled—till conquered by their own brethren, they yielded what they had so bravely struggled to retain. Since then, tradition informs us, they were called " the Elder Brothers," on account of their conquest of the Hurons. The dispersion which took place in the year 1648, gave the victors possession of all (now) Canada West.

The Iroquois overcame their brethren soon after the

introduction of European fire arms, and it was the dread
of these weapons which in part induced them to seek
shelter amid the tribes on the south-west shores of Lake
Huron. The first Nation fled to the South of Lake
Huron, about Saganaw—subsequently it moved further
South on the St. Clair. The second Nation went to
the North-west, at the foot of the great lake called
Kechegum, now called Lake Superior. Of the third,
a great number were adopted by their conquerors
in perfect amity. The remaining two Nations joined
with western tribes, and in the course of time have
nearly lost their nationality.

The exultation of the Iroquois was almost beyond
bounds. They pursued their retreating brethren over
the St. Clair, and along the Northern shores of Lake
Huron. They were the possessors of the whole territory; the valley of the Ottawa yielded them their
game, which a few years before was the right and support of their exiled brethren.

Dejected, disheartened, the Hurons presented themselves at the doors of the Great Council Wigwams of
different Nations, whom they had made enemies by their
former repeated depredations, but rather than submit to
be led by their own brethren, as a conquered race
throughout their former possessions, those who went to

the north-west called a council among themselves, in which it was determined upon what should be done.

This council, according to ancient tradition, must have been held at the outlet of French River, and on the Northern shore of Lake Huron.

The Hurons assembled themselves in council, and in the course of their deliberations, they desired several of their Chiefs to visit the great Ojibway family on Lake Superior, and see whether that people would forgive them the wrongs they had done them, and admit them as their allies.

The war canoes of the Hurons were manned and paddled on the bosom of the great lake in search of a place of refuge. They arrived quite late in the autumn at the eastermost village of the Ojibways, a situation they named *Pe-quak-qua-wah-ming*, (Round Point,) near the fork of a bay called by the French Aunce Bay, now known as *Ke-wa-o-non*.

It was the policy of the Hurons to present themselves in a pitiable condition before their superiors, the Ojibway family of the great lake, that they might the more easily obtain their favor and sympathy. Tradition informs us that they came and presented themselves before the Council-door of that Nation, and begged them to spare their own children's lives. They had painted their faces black, rent their clothes, and with emaciated and haggard frames, came to implore their aid. They narrated their misfortunes, to incite the pity of the nation. The Ojibways saw them, and yielded to pity and compassion. The Hurons were received as friends; they overcame the war spirit of the Ojibways, who kindly seated them at their side.

The Huron Chief detailed the barbarous acts of their brethren, and narrated in glowing language their cruelty. That their allies had driven them from their lands ; that their children had been thrown on the blaze of their own fires in their own wigwams, and the wigwams beneath which they had resided for years, reduced to ashes !— Some were compelled to drink the blood of their own children, while those who were carried away into their own brethren's country, were denied food, and were offered their own children's flesh in its stead.

That country was covered with blood, and with the mangled remains of their fathers who had fought for their lands. The exulting cry of the Oneida, mingled with the shouts of the Mohawk, was heard in the land where once they lived. They said that the graves of their people were desecrated, and that the bodies of many of their women and children lay unburied on their battle-fields, from the waters of Erie to the valley of Ottawa in the North. The Hurons related the account of their children's massacre with tears and sobs, and by such means moved those who had been their enemies to pity them, and kindled in the hearts of some a feeling of revenge upon the Iroquois, who had so recklessly overstepped the barrier which Nature hath raised in the hearts of all men. If thus the fugitive Hurons had gone to solicit aid in the midst of the Ojibway country, they could have aroused the bravery of the Nation to have gone in arms in their favor, and carried on war still longer.

At this time there lived the greatest of renowned warriors, *Wah-boo-geeg*, who dwelt at *Pequakqua-wah-ming*. His name has been handed down from generation to generation, and his bravery and fame been envied by all young warriors.

It is said that this *Wah-boo-geeg* arose in the council with a club in his hand, and remembering the Hurons and their many barbarous acts, shook the war club over their heads, and said that it was not fear which had led them to give them such a reception, but it was pity for their innocent children, that induced them to open their arms and receive them. He told them that henceforward none should molest—that their children and the children of his own people should sport together—that

the war club of the Ojibways should protect them—and
that they were as numerous as the leaves of the forest
trees, towards the setting sun.

A situation was assigned them near by where they
and their children could reside, and be near the villages
of the Ojibways.   It was adjacent to a bay about fifteen
miles eastward of .Alluce Bay, and a river whose
name has been Huron from that day to this.

I have been thus particular in naming the events
which led to the subjugation of the *Huron Iroquois* by
their own brethren, the Iroquois of the East, that the
reader may be informed of the chief cause of their subsequent success, which was the fact of their having
enlisted in their favor the Ojibway Nation.   The Western Iroquois, finding a refuge in the midst of Western
tribes, endeavored to stop the commerce which had been
commenced by the great Ottawa river, and profitably
carried on between the French and the Ojibways of
Lake Superior.   This rash attempt on the part of the
Iroquois brought on the disastrous war between that
Nation and the Ojibways, an account of which is reserved for the next chapter.

CHAPTER VII.

" In peace there's nothing so becomes a man
As modest stillness and humanity ;
But when the blast of war blows in his ears,
Then imitates the action of the tiger."

Before the dispersion of the Hurons no difficulty existed between the Ojibways and the Eastern Iroquois,
but the Western Hurons often waylaid the hunters of
the Ojibway Nation, and continuing so to do eventually
aroused the war-whoop of revenge far and near.

After the year 1608, Champlain traders began to carry
on their commercial transactions on the waters of the
Mahahmoo Sebee, (Trading River,) which introduced
among the Indians fire-arms woollen-goods. and steel
for weapons of war.

The next year (1609,) Champlain made a treaty with
6

the Northern tribes, an examination of which will
show in what manner they were to aid them in
their wars with the Iroquois.   History exhibits the
disastrous results following this connection with
them.

During a period of thirty-five years the Ojibways on
Lake Superior, had been obtaining fire-arms from the
French of Quebec.   They carried on a peaceful traffic
with the French of Lake Superior until the year 1652,
when the troubles between the Iroquois and the Ojibways commenced.   The commerce which for thirty-five
years had received no interruption, either from quarrels
without or dissentions within their midst, was attacked
by the Iroquois, who barbarously plundered and massacred the Ojibway warriors, who had been out for Montreal to barter furs for domestic goods, as also for weapons of war and fire-water.   At the entrance of French
River, two of this company escaped from the Iroquois,
and conveyed an account of the fate of their comrades
to the Ojibways at Aunce Bay.   This so incensed the
Algonquin tribe that they sent the invaders a message
to this effect, that if they ever perpetrated the like again,
they would send a few of their warriors in pursuit, to
exterminate them.   The proud Iroquois laughed in
scorn at the threat of the Ojibways, and sent to learn

whether the Ojibways included their women in their proposed extermination.

A Council of Peace was called by the Ojibways, which was held, according to tradition, below Sault St. Marie, at a place called in the Algonquin tongue, *Massessanga.* This council received the deputies of the Iroquois, who concluded a treaty, which they secretly intended not to preserve.

During the summer all lived in peace. They met as friends on the shores of the Huron, and as friends hunted in the valley of the Ottawa.

A second offence was committed on the Ojibways, above the Falls, near where Bytown now stands, on the Ottawa River. The Iroquois fell upon a party of the Ojibways, who were hauling their canoes over the carrying place. These they took from them, as also their " fire-water," which they had obtained from the French. About twenty were slain ; the remaining swam across the river before their enemies could reach them. Of these, two died on their way home, from hunger and exposure. The rest, three in number, only survived to reach the South shore of Lake Superior, and give information of the attack. The Ojibways were highly exasperated. They were excited to fury, and a desire for revenge reigned in every heart.

F

The Hurons availed themselves of this favorable opportunity to remind them that they had suffered like
cruelties from their brethren.   Another Council was to
be called.   The Chiefs of the Ojibways were to go to
Nahtooway, *Sahgeeny*, the principal village of the Iroquois, on the easternmost shore of Lake Huron.

They arrived during an Iroquois scalp dance of triumph.   It was over the scalps of people of their own
nation.   For several days they knew not whether they
would be massacred or allowed to return; they could
get no satisfaction.   The sages of the Iroquois knowing
however that their people had aggrieved the feelings of
the Ojibways, wisely concluded to reflect seriously upon
the importance of pressing peace with so powerful a
Nation as the Ojibways were universally acknowledged
to be.   They met the Ojibway Chief in council, who
demanded of them as many packs of furs as warriors
they had slain, which the Iroquois Chiefs granted amid
the manifest dissatisfaction of the people.

The council agreed that the treaty should never be
infringed upon, and that it should be held inviolate and
permanent.   It was a fair, impartial, and open treaty,
and it was distinctly understood that the first breach of
it should be a signal for war between the offenders and
the offended.

They scrutinized the features of one and another—shook hands, and bade each other farewell,—(a *final* farewell.)

The Chiefs of the Ojibways returned to their own country. Trade was again prosecuted with renewed energy and enterprise, and several valuable loads of furs were sent to the whites of Montreal. No shock of discord was heard,—the shrill war-whoop was hushed. Peace dwelt among the mountains of the North.

Without fear the Ojibway and Iroquois hunters met, and spent their evenings together, relating each his adventures and exploits. The Ottawa river was thickly dotted with canoes heavily freighted with furs from the North and West. Blankets were bought with these, and fire-water, which was carried to the extreme end of Lake Superior, and to its Northern shores.

The Hurons became so forgetful of their late wars, that they even ventured to accompany the trading Indians (now called Ottawas) down to Montreal, and for one year and a summer they suffered no molestation—all was quiet. The Iroquois saw that the French were more friendly to the Indians of Lake Superior than they were to them ; and that the Ojibways were a protection to those by whom they were formerly molested.

The treaty had remained unbroken nearly three years

when bands of the Iroquois waylaid the Ojibways simultaneously at various points on the *Mah-ah-moo-sebee.* The news of these unprovoked attacks reached the shores of Lake Superior, but as it was late in the fall, they deemed it imprudent to proceed against the Iroquois, and delayed their expedition until the ensuing spring.

Runners were sent during the winter to the different allies of the Ojibways, the Sacs and Foxes, Menomones, Kinnestenoes, Pottawatamies, and the Hurons of Sandusky, each of whom were informed of the movements of the great Ojibway family in the West.

Strings of wampum were sent from village to village by fleet runners from the extreme end of Lake Superior to the South, far over the prairies of Illinois. The bays of Michigan resounded with the war cry of the Sacs, while the Menomones trained their young warriors for the approaching conflict.

The war dance became a constant exercise, and in fact, the chief amusement of the Indians. The Hurons excited the revengeful feelings of the Ojibways by telling them of the outrages the Iroquois had committed on their children. They shook their war clubs towards the rising sun, and a signal was given that betokened a terrific onslaught. Their hunting grounds were abandoned, and their women who had attended the cornfields were obliged to fish during the summer, in order to obtain a subsistence.

By previous arrangement, the warriors of the Nations were to meet below Sault St. Marie, at the first chang-ing of the flower moon (May).

The time arrived. Wah-boo-jeeg's son mustered the war canoes before the point of *Peguahquawom*, near the outlet of a deep bay on the South shore of Lake Superior. When the voices of the war chiefs announced the time of preparation to an eager multitude, a deafening shout arose to heaven, and awoke the echoing spirit of the forest. The rattling of the mysterious Waskeinzke (Deer's Whoof), and the beating of the drum were heard. The tramp of the furious Ojibways and Hurons shook the earth as they danced around the blaze of their council fires.

In the morning, at dawn, the war canoes from Shah-gahwahmik (the point) were in sight; near Kewaowon two hundred of them approached!

The Sahsahquon (war cry) and song were heard in the distance from over the waters. Never had the wa-ters been agitated by so great a fleet of canoes. The muscular arm of the warriors propelled the canoes with rapid speed on their way.

In former times the old Chief, Wah-boo-jeeg, led the

warrior bands in person, but being quite aged, he committed the charge to his son, *Naiquod.* The old Chief expressed his approbation of the expedition against the Iroquois, by standing near the edge of a rock which was partially suspended over the waters—from which commanding position he addressed the warriors who were in their canoes ready to go eastward.

I propose in the following chapter to give you the speech of Wah-boo-jeeg to the assembled warriors, and an account of those battles which terminated in the subjugation of the Eastern Iroquois, and of the places at which they were fought.

CHAPTER VIII.

In the last chapter we left Wah-boo-jeeg standing upon an overhanging cliff. For a moment he gazed around upon the war-clad throng in canoes before him, then spoke to them as follows :—

"When I was young, the Nahtoowassee of the West was heard from hill to hill. They were as many as the forest trees, but because they had smoked the pipe of peace when their hearts were not right, the Monedoo they disobeyed, sent our fathers to drive them from our lands, near a lake in the West they called Esahyah-mahday (Knife Lake), and they fled West of the father of rivers to dwell in the habitations of strangers. I was the assistant of my father during these bloody wars.— Go, now, at the rising of the sun. The Iroquois have filled the land with blood, and the same Monedoo who was with me on the Western plains will be with you to prosper and preserve you." A shout arose. "Go," he added, "with your war clubs—make a straight path to the wigwam of the pale face, and demand the land of the weeping Huron. I will sit upon the edge of this rock, and await your return."

The old man sat down, and the canoes moved Eastward, in search of the foe. The Western shore of Michigan was also thronged by the canoes of the Menomonies, Pottawatamies, Sacks and Foxes,—the Southern Hurons came with other tribes across the St. Clair, and overran the South.

Tradition informs us that seven hundred canoes met at Kewetawahonning, one party of whom was to take the route to Mahamooseebee, the second towards Wahweyagahmah, (now Lake Simcoe), the third was to take the route towards the river St. Clair, and meet the Southern Hurons. I will here remark that they had several reasons for waging war against the Iroquois.— First, for having broke the last treaty of peace by the murder of some of their warriors ; second, to clear the way of trade between the Ojibways and the French, (the Iroquois then lived along the Ottawa river), and third, to regain the land of the Western Hurons, and, if possible, drive the Iroquois wholly from the peninsula.

The warriors who took the Mahamooseebee, had several engagements with them, but outnumbering them, they easily routed the Iroquois. Those who had gone to the St. Clair had likewise a fierce battle at the mouth of a river called by the Algonquins, Sahgeeng, and afterwards being joined by the Southern Hurons, overran the whole of the South of the peninsula.

The most bloody battles were fought on Lake Simcoe, at a place called Ramma, at Mud Lake, Pigeon Lake, and Rice Lake : the last that was fought took place at the mouth of the river Trent.

Forty years had nearly elapsed since the Hurons had been routed, but they had not forgotten the land of their birth—the places that were once so dear to them. The thought of regaining their former possessions inspired them with a courage that faced every danger. They fought like tigers.

The first battle between the Ojibways and the Eastern Iroquois or Mohawks, was fought at a place near where Orillea is now situated, about one-quarter of a mile Northward. The Mohawks collected in great numbers here, and awaited the attack of the Western Hurons and Ojibways. They resisted stoutly for three days—at the close of which, tradition informs us, they sued for mercy, which was granted, and the few survivors were allowed to go to Lake Huron, where they remained during the rest of the war.

The second battle of any account was fought at Pigeon Lake, where the Iroquois had made a strong fort, remains of which are to be seen at this day. At this place great numbers of the Ojibways were killed. For a time the result was doubtful, but finally the Ojibways took the fort by storm, and but few of the Iroquois were spared.

The third battle was fought near Mud Lake, about twelve miles North of Peterboro. Not a male person was spared, and the next day another village that stood on the present site of Peterboro and Smithtown, was attacked, and an immense number slaughtered.

I will not attempt to narrate the many barbarous acts which took place on both sides, for humanity shudders at the bare thought of them. They spared none. It is said that they fought the last few who resisted, on a shoal in the river with arrows, strings and other missiles ; that their blood dyed the water, and their bodies filled the stream.

From both banks of the river the wail of woe and grief arose from the orphan children, whose loud cries and sobs were heard far distant. Here side by side the hostile warriors rolled in blood and agony, while the eagles, buzzards, and crows, flying round and round, added their screech to the noise of the combatants, and by their actions testified their joy that a day of general feasting had arrived. Their

"Slaughter heaped on high its weltering ranks."

Death made a throne of the bodies of the slain, and arm in arm with his hand in hand, friend Despair ascended and ruled the day.

The fourth village which they attacked was at the mouth of the Otonabee, on Rice Lake, where several hundreds were slain. The bodies were in two heaps : one of which was the slain of the Iroquois ; the other of the Ojibways.

Panic-struck the Iroquois collected their remaining forces in Percy, now Lewis's Farm, where for two days and nights they fought like wild beasts. Their shrieks and shouts were heard on each side of the river Trent, so madly did they rush upon destruction.

Of this band of warriors, one alone was saved. The women and children were spared to wander in solitary anguish, and mourn over husbands and fathers whose bones were before them,—sad memorials of desolating war. At this day arms of various descriptions are to be found, such as war-clubs, axes, spears, knives, arrow-heads and tomahawks scattered with human bones.

The fifth and last battle was fought on an island

near the mouth of the river Trent, where most of the canoes had collected. At early dawn the warriors landed, and with one wild, fierce rush, commenced their work of havoc and extermination.

Yells and groans were heard on every side,—hand to hand they fought, and those who attempted to fly were pursued into the water and there slain and scalped.

When the news of these victories reached the Mohawks, they were incredulous, but soon learned that the Iroquois were entirely broken up and the country subdued.

The war-whoop of the trading Indians and their host abounded. Reveling and feasting celebrated the downfall of the Iroquois. In vain the Iroquois, who remained, sent to the French, suing for peace. The petitions were not heeded, and they vainly attempted to regain by scattered skirmishes a foot-hold on the land they were destined soon after to abandon forever.

They returned from Canada, and their conquerors allotted them places of habitation. The Shawnees occupied the Southern, and the Ottaways and Ojibways the Northern parts.

Peace was then restored, and the confines of Niagara and St. Lawrence reaped its benefits.

This took place about 1666, and continued for six years, when the French undertook to lay the foundation of a fort near the foot of Lake Ontario, called in the Algonquin language, Kah-tah-nah-queng, (Cataraque).

Several attempts have since been made by the elder brethren to renew their vengeance against the French, Ottaways and Ojibways, also to regain their former possessions, but they were unable to succeed, for the whole of the western tribes had combined against them, and they were utterly subdued by overpowering numbers.

Recently the Mohawks, a part of the Six Nations, have settled in Grand River, and others in Bay Quinty, back of Adolphustown, from the American side, they having been engaged with the British in the wars of that nation.

It is somewhat remarkable that those who now live near Adolphustown, Canada West, still adhere to old customs and usages, though the Rev. Mr. Givins has done a great deal towards introducing among them the arts of civilized life.

These nations used to send their warriors on the waters of the *Sa-ga-naw* of the north, Ottawa river, Lake Huron and Sandusky, away west to the prairies of Illi·

nois and the waters of Green Bay, as also to the shores
of Lake Superior. On the east to the White Mountains
of Vermont,—down the Delaware river and the upper
branches of the Ohio.

Their war path was drenched with the blood of their
enemies all around them. They were, in fact, the
Turks of the American Forest. By degrees they have
fallen before the rapidly increasing numbers of their
enemies. What war has not done, strong drink has,
until now they are a weak and puny race.

The pale face says that there is a fate hanging over
the Indian bent on his destruction. Preposterous!—
They give him liquors to destroy himself with, and then
charge the great Good Spirit as the author of their misery and mortality.

The arm of the Iroquois warrior wields the war-club
no more. A few of his children are now peacefully
following the plough in Canada and in Western New-
York, while others of them mingle with those tribes
against whom the war-cry of their Nation was once
raised. They now live in amity and peace, and hail
the dawning of a better day.

CHAPTER IX.

THEIR LEGENDARY STORIES AND HISTORICAL TALES.

" 'Tis a story,
Handed from ages down ; a nurse's tale,
Which cilhdren open-eyed and mouthed devour,
And thus as garrulous ignorance relates,
We learn it and believe —————,"

THE Ojibways have a great number of legends, stories, and historical tales, the relating and hearing of
which, form a vast fund of winter evening instruction
and amusement.

There is not a lake or mountain that has not connected with it some story of delight or wonder, and nearly
every beast and bird is the subject of the story-teller,
being said to have transformed itself at some prior time
into some mysterious formation—of men going to live
in the stars, and of imaginary beings in the air, whose
rushing passage roars in the distant whirlwinds.

I have known some Indians who would commence
to narrate legends and stories in the month of October
and not end until quite late in the spring, sometimes
not till quite late in the month of May, and on every
evening of this long term tell a new story.

Some of these stories are most exciting, and so intensely interesting, that I have seen children during their
relation, whose tears would flow quite plentifully, and
their breasts heave with thoughts too big for utterance.

Night after night for weeks have I sat and eagerly
listened to these stories.   The days following, the characters would haunt me at every step, and every moving
leaf would seem to be a voice of a spirit.   To those
days I look back with pleasurable emotions.   Many of
these fanciful stories have been collected by H. R.
Schoolcraft, Esq.

It is not my purpose to unnecessarily extend this
work with a large number of these.   I will, however,
in this connection narrate a few, in order to give you
some idea of the manner in which my people amuse
themselves in their wigwams, and promise to send you,
at some future day, a good handfull from the forest.

These legends have an important bearing on the
character of the children of our Nation.   The fire-blaze
is endeared to them in after years by a thousand happy

recollections. By mingling thus, social habits are formed and strengthened. When the hour for this recrea-
tion arrives, they lay down the bow and the arrow and
joyously repair to the wigwam of the aged man of the
village, who is always ready to accommodate the
young.

Legends are of three distinct classes, namely, the
Amusing, the Historical, and the Moral. In the Fall
we have one class, in the Winter another, and in the
Spring a third. I can at present have only time and
space to give specimens of the second of these.

LEGEND FIRST.

THE STAR AND THE LILY.

An old chieftain sat in his wigwam quietly smoking
his favorite pipe, when a crowd of Indian boys and girls
suddenly entered, and with numerous offerings of tobacco, begged him to tell them a story. Then the old
man began :—

" There was once a time when this world was filled
with happy people, when all nations were as one, and
the crimson tide of war had not begun to roll. Plenty
of game was in the forest and on the plains. None

G

were in want, for a full supply was at hand. Sickness •
was unknown.   The beasts of the field were tame, they
came and went at the bidding of man.   One unending
spring gave no place for winter—for its cold blasts or
its unhealthy chills.   Every tree and bush yielded
fruit.

Flowers carpeted the earth ; the air was laden with
their fragrance, and redolent with the songs of married
warblers, that flew from branch to branch, fearing none,
for there were none to harm them.   There were birds
then of more beautiful song and plumage than now.

It was at such a time, when earth was a paradise and
man worthily its possessor, that the Indians were the
lone inhabitants of the American wilderness.

They numbered millions, and living as Nature de-
signed them to live, enjoyed its many blessings.   Instead of amusements in close rooms, the sports of the
fields were theirs.   At night they met on the wide green
fields.   They watched the stars ; they loved to gaze at
them, for they believed them to be the residences of the
good who had been taken home by the Great Spirit.

One night they saw one star that shone brighter than
all others.   Its location was far away in the South near
a mountain peak.   For many nights it was seen, till at
length it was doubted by many that the star was as far

distant in the Southern skies as it seemed to be. This doubt led to an examination, which proved the star to be only a short distance, and near the tops of some trees.

A number of warriors were deputed to go and see what it was. They went, and on their return said it appeared strange and somewhat like a bird. A committee of the wise men were called to inquire into, and if possible ascertain the meaning of the strange phenomena.

They feared that it might be the omen of some disaster. Some thought it precursor of good, others of evil, and some supposed it to be the star spoken of by their forefathers, as the forerunner of a dreadful war.

One moon had nearly gone by, and yet the mystery remained unsolved.

One night a young warrior had a dream, in which a beautiful maiden came and stood at his side, and thus addressed him :

'Young brave ! charmed with the land of thy forefathers, its flowers, its birds, its rivers, its beautiful lakes, and its mountains clothed with green, I have left my sisters in yonder world to dwell among you. Young brave ! ask your wise and your great men where I can live and see the happy race continually ;

ask them what form I shall assume in order to be loved.'

Thus discoursed the bright stranger. The young man awoke. On stepping out of his lodge he saw the star yet blazing in its accustomed place.

At early dawn the Chief's crier was sent round the camp to call every warrior to the Council Lodge. When they had met, the young warrior related his dream.— They concluded that the star that had been seen in the South had fallen in love with mankind, and that it was desirous to dwell with them.

The next night five tall, noble-looking, adventurous braves were sent to welcome the stranger to earth.— They went and presented to it a pipe of peace, filled with sweet scented herbs, and were rejoiced to find that it took it from them. As they returned to the village, the star with expanded wing followed, and hovered over their homes till the dawn of day.

Again it came to the young man in a dream, and desired to know where it should live, and what form it should take.

Places were named. On the top of giant trees, or in flowers. At length it was told to choose a place itself, and it did so.

At first, it dwelt in the white rose of the mountains;

but there it was so buried that it could not be seen. It went to the prairie, but it feared the hoof of the buffalo. It next sought the rocky cliff, but there it was so high, that the children whom it loved most could not see it.

' I know where I shall live,' said the bright fugitive, " where I can see the gliding canoe of the race I most admire. Children ! yes, they shall be my playmates, and I will kiss their brows when they slumber by the side of cool lakes. The nations shall love me wherever I am.'

These words having been said, she alighted on the waters where she saw herself reflected. The next morning, thousands of white flowers were seen on the surface of the lakes, and the Indians gave them this name — ' *Wah-be-gwon-nee*,' (White Lily.) Now," continued the old man, " this star lived in the Southern skies. Its brethren can be seen far off in the cold North, hunting the great bear, whilst its sisters watch her in the East and West.

" Children ! when you see the lily on the waters, take it in your hands, and hold it to the skies, that it may be happy on earth as its two sisters, the morning and evening stars, are happy in heaven."

While tears fell fast from the eyes of all, the old man laid down and was soon silent in sleep.

Since that, I have often plucked the white lily, and garlanded it around my head—have dipped it in its watery bed—but never have I seen it without remem bering the legend of the descending star.

———

LEGEND SECOND,

HISTORICAL—THE LONG CHASE.

THE Indian warrior of days long past, thought that distance should never be considered when he went forth to war, provided he was certain of winning the applause of his fellows. Fatigue and hunger were alike looked upon as minor matters, and were endured without a murmur.

The long continued wars which once existed between the Ojibways and the Iroquois, gave rise to the following legend, which was originally related to me by an Ojibway Chief, whose name was Na-nah-boo-sho.

A party of six Iroquois runners had been sent by their leading Chiefs from Ke-wa-we-won, on the Southern shore of Lake Superior, to examine the position of the Ojibways, who were supposed to be on the island called Moo-ne-quah-na-kaung-ning. The spies having arrived opposite the island on which their enemies had encamp-

ed, (which was about three miles from the main shore)
built a war canoe with the bark of an elm tree, launched
it at the hour of midnight, and having implored the god
of war to smile upon them and keep the lake in peace,
landed on the island, and were soon prowling through
the village of the unconscious Ojibway. They were so
cautious in all their movements, that their footsteps did
not even awaken the sleeping dogs.

It happened, however, that they were discovered, and
that too by a young woman, who according to an ancient custom was leading a solitary life previous to becoming a mother. In her wakefulness, she saw them
pass near her lodge, and heard them speak, yet could
not understand their words, though she thought them
to be of the Na-do-way tribe.

When they had passed, she stole out of her own wigwam to that of her aged grand-mother, to whom she related what she had seen and heard. The aged woman
only reprimanded her daughter for her imprudence and
did not heed her words.

" But, mother," replied the girl, " I speak the truth ;
the dreaded Na-do-ways are in our village, and if the
warriors of the Buffalo race do not heed the story of a
foolish girl, their women and their children must perish."

The words of the girl were finally believed, and the

warriors of the Crane and Buffalo tribes prepared themselves for a conflict.

The war-whoop echoed to the sky—and the rattling
of bows and arrows was heard in every part of the island.
In about one hour the main shore was lined with about
eight hundred canoes, the occupants of which were
anxiously awaiting the appearance of the spies. These
desperate men, however, had made up their mind to ply
their oars to the utmost, and as the day was breaking,
they launched their canoes from a woody cove, shot
round the island, and started in the direction of the
Porcupine Mountains, which were about sixty miles
distant. As soon as they came in sight of the Ojibways, the latter became quite frantic, and giving their
accustomed yell, the whole multitude started after them
as swift as the flight of birds.

The waters of the mighty lake were without a ripple,
other than that made by the swiftly gliding canoe, and
the beautiful fish moved among their rocky haunts in
perfect peace, unconscious of the chase above.

The Iroquois were some two miles ahead, and while
they strained every nerve for life, one voice rose high
in the air, bearing an invocation to the spirits of their
race for protection. In answer to their prayer, a thick
fog fell upon the water and caused great confusion.—

One of the Ojibway warriors laid down his paddle, seized his mysterious rattle (made of deer's hoof) and in a strange, wild song, implored the spirits of his race to clear away the fog, that they might pursue their enemies. The burden of their song was—

> " Mon-e-doo ne bah bah me tah wah
> Ke shig ne bah bah me tah goon,
> Ne bee ne wah wah goom me goon,
> Ne ke che dah—awas, awas."

Which may be translated as follows :—

> "Spirits ! whom we have always obeyed,
> Here cause the sky now to obey ;
> Place now the waters all in our power,
> We are warriors—away, away."

As the last strain of music departed, the fog rolled away, and the Iroquois spies were seen hastening to the shore, near Montreal River. Then came the fog again and then departed, in answer to the conflicting prayers of the two nations. Long and exciting was the race. But the Great Spirit was the friend of the Ojibways— and just as the Iroquois were landing on the beach, four of them were pierced with arrows, and the remaining two taken prisoners. A council was then called for the purpose of determining what should be done with them, and it was determined that they should be tortured at the stake. They were, accordingly, fastened to a tree, and surrounded with wood, when just as the flaming torch was to be applied, an aged warrior stepped forth from the crowd of spectators, and thus addressed the assembly :—

"Why are you to destroy these men? They are brave warriors, but not more distinguished than we are. We can gain no benefit from their death. Why not let them live, that they may go and tell their people of our power, and that our warriors are as numerous as the stars of the Northern sky?"

The Council pondered upon the old man's advice, and in the breasts of each there was a struggle between their love of revenge and their love of glory. Both were victorious.

One of the spies was released, and as he ascended a narrow valley, leading to the Porcupine Mountains, the fire was applied to the dry wood piled around the form of the other, and in the darkness of midnight and amid the shouting of his cruel enemies, the body of the Iroquois prisoner was reduced to ashes.

The spot where the sacrifice took place has been riven by many a thunderbolt since that eventful hour, for the god of war was displeased with the faint-heartedness of the Ojibways for valuing a man more highly than the privilege of revenge ; and the summer of the next year that saw the remains of the humane Ojibway buried on the shore of Lake Superior, saw also the remains of the pardoned spy consigned to the earth on the shore of Michigan.

Thus ends the legion of Shah-gah-wah-mik, one of the Apostle Islands, which the French named La Pointe, and which was originally known as Mo-ne-quon-a-koning. The village stood where the old trading.establishment was located, and among the greenest of the graves now seen in the hamlet of La Pointe is that of the Indian girl who exposed herself to reproach for the purpose of saving her people.

————

TALES.

LEGEND THIRD.

THE THUNDER'S NEST.

The following legend will impart some instruction relative to the Indian idea of thunder.

Once upon a time when no wars existed among men, the only thing they feared was a great bird seen flying through the air during moonlight nights. When it was seen in the day time its presence was usually followed by the visitation of some great misfortune upon any one who should chance to see it.

These monstrous birds were supposed to have their nests somewhere, and great curiosity existed to know its location, as well as to know somewhat of the nature of the bird ; but no one seemed fortunate enough to discover the resort of these great birds which were called *Ah-ne-me-keeg*, (Thunders.)

There lived on the northern shore of Lake Superior an Indian warrior who from his childhood had been noted for being a wise and sedate man ; it was supposed by many that he would some day go on a great exploit, as none was like him for courage, wisdom and prudence. As he was returning from one of his hunting expeditions, the night came on sooner than he expected it would, and darkness gathered around him while he was a great distance from his home. On his way he was obliged to traverse the ice on lake and river. The moon shone as clear and perfect as it had ever shone to light a traveller's path. On the warrior's back was a beaver, and in his hand the tried and trusted spear, with which he had captured it. As he was crossing the last lake the shadow of some great object passed before him, and he soon saw approaching a great bird, which in a moment caught him and all he had, and arose. The bird carried him westward, far above the earth, yet not so far as to prevent him from seeing it, and the doings upon it. After travelling a great distance, they came in view of a high hill, which was barren of trees, but bore one bold barren rock. As they neared it, the bird endeavored to dash him upon its side, but the old Indian so placed his spear that he was not injured in the least degree. At length he was thrown upon the place where the young birds were. He heard fierce muttering thunder overhead, and found himself left to the mercy of the wild birds.

Soon after, they began to peck his head, when he, thinking them helpless, ventured to make battle with them. The Indian arose, and soon found they were too much for him. Whenever they winked, a flash of lightning would pass from their eyes and scorch him so severely as to burn his hands and face.

The birds were quite small, and not able to execute much, and therefore by perseverance he gained the mastery over them with his spear. He dragged one of them to the edge, rolled it over the precipice, and took the skin from the other.

On looking round, he discovered that he was near the North-west end of Lake Superior; he then threw the other carcase from him, and after filling his pipe with

Ke-ne-ke-nik (tobacco), taking one or two whiffs he held it in his hand, and pointing with its stem to the four corners of the heaven, he offered up a prayer, which he believed was heard. He then got inside of the young thunder skin, sewed himself in it, and rolled down the rocks. As he tumbled from rock to rock, the feathers of the skin would flash with fire. After descending about half way to the bottom of the precipice, the skin in which he was bound bore him on its wings, and after a long flight, alighted with him near the spot from whence he was taken ten days before. His wife and children were in mourning for his loss, for they had seen him taken from the ice, and were convinced that he had been taken by some mysterious spirit. As might be supposed, when he returned he surprised them by bringing to his children the hearts of the young thunders.— He broiled them, and as he did so, the fire made a crackling noise.*

The next summer, the mountains West of the Me-she-be-goo-toong, on the borders of Lake Superior, were continually enveloped in flames and heavy clouds, for it is there that the remainder of the thunder birds rested.

Since mankind have gone in great crowds, these birds

---

* Indian children are now told that when the fire makes a noise, the hearts of young thunders are broiling in it.

are seldom seen, but are often heard in the skies, where they fly higher than they once did. Once they lived on human flesh, but now they subsist on the wild game of the forest. They wink, and the fire flashes from their eyes. Their nests are now built on the Ah-sen-wah-ge-wing (Rocky Mountains), in the far West, and at times they are heard passing through the air towards the East, on their way to the sea, for they live upon fish and serpents, since they have been subdued by man.

LEGEND FOURTH.

THE TWO COUSINS.

THERE lived amongst the hills of the North, two most intimate friends, who had appeared to have loved each other from the years of their earliest childhood.—In summer they lived by a beautiful lake. In autumn on the banks of a noble river. In personal appearance they were very near alike ; they were of the same age and statue. In their early days a good old Indian wo-man attended to their wants, and cared for tl eir wig-wams; together they strolled among the green woods, and shared the results of their ramblings. Years flitted by. Manhood came, when they used large bows and arrows.

One day the old lady took them by her side, and told them that the Nation to which they belonged held a fast, and that she wanted them to fast that they might become great hunters. And they did fast.

As spring advanced, they killed a great many wild ducks, and kept the old woman of the wigwam busy in taking care of their game.

In the latter part of the year they killed a great number of beaver, with the furs of which they clothed their grand-mother and themselves.

In their journey one day, they made an agreement to this effect, that if the gods should make known any manifest favor to the one he should inform the other.

In the fall, they were far from the rivers, but yet moved towards the North, where they knew the bears most resorted. During that winter they killed a great many, as also during the ensuing March.

At the close of one of their hunting expeditions, they turned their feet towards home, at which they arrived at a late hour. As they approached, they heard the sound of several voices beside that of their grand-mother. They listened, and discovered that strangers were in their wigwam. They entered, and beheld two young and beautiful damsels seated in that part of the room in which they generally rested during the night.

The hunters and the young women appeared very strange and modest. At length the old lady said to the young men :—

"Noo-se-se-took ! My children, I have called these two young women from the South, that they may aid me in taking care of all the meat and venison you may bring home, for I am getting old and weak and cannot do as much as I used to. I have put them by your sides that they may be your companions."

When the last words were spoken, they looked upon each other, and soon left, to wander by themselves in the forest.

They there consulted together as to whether they should comply with her request. One said he should leave the wigwam. The other said that if they left, there would be no one to supply their aged grand-mother; and they finally agreed to remain in the wigwam and pay no regard to the new comers.

They slept side by side every night, and agreed that if either should wish to love one of the young strangers he would inform the other, and that they would then separate forever. In February they obtained a vast amount of game ; the bears having returned to their winter quarters were easily found and captured

It was observed that one of the young men gazed

H

very intently at one of the strangers, and the next morning as they went out, he asked the other whether he did not begin to love the young damsel who sat on his side of the birchen fire. He replied negatively. It was true that one of the cousins appeared to be deeply absorbed in thought every evening, and that his manner was quite reserved.

After a fortunate hunting day, as they were wending their way home with their heavy burden of bear and deer, one accused the other of loving the young woman. " Tell me," said he, " and if you do, I will leave you to yourselves. If you have a wife, I cannot enjoy your company, or take the same delight with you as I do when we follow the chase."

His cousin sighed, and said—" I will tell you to-night as we lie side by side."

At night they conversed together, and agreed to hunt, and if they did not meet with success, they would separate. The next morning they went to the woods,— they were not a great distance from each other during the hunt. The one who was in love shot only five, while the other returned with the tongues of twenty bears. The former was all the time thinking of the damsel at home, while the latter thought only of his game, having nothing else to divert his mind.

On their return, the lucky man informed the grand-mother that he should leave the next morning, and that what he should kill on the morrow must be searched after, as he should not return to tell them where he had killed the game. His cousin was grieved to find that his mind was made up to leave, and began to expostulate with him to change his determination; but he would not be persuaded to do so.

The next day came. The young man who was to leave, bound a rabbit skin about his neck to keep it warm, and having used on himself red and yellow paints, left. His cousin followed close in his rear, entreating him not to leave him.

" I will go," said he, " and live in the North, where I shall see but few persons, and when you come that way, you will see me."

They walked side by side, until the departing cousin began to ascend—and as he did so, the other wept the more bitterly, and entreated him most perseveringly not to go.

The cousin ascended to the skies, and is seen in the North, *Ke-wa-den-ah-mung* (North Star), still hunting the bear ; while the other wept himself to nought before he could arrive home, and now he answers and mocks every body. He lives in the craggy rocks and deep woods, and his name is *Bah-swa-way* (Echo). The young maidens lived for a long time in the South, under ambrosial bowers, awaiting the return of their lovers, until one fell in love with another, and the other is waiting for the return of her lover, where

> " She looks as clear as morning roses,
> Newly washed in dew."

AN HISTORICAL TALE.

THE EFFECTS OF LIQUOR.

A FEW years after the extermination of the Iroquois from the peninsula which is formed by the three lakes, Huron, Erie and Ontario, a free and uninterrupted intercourse existed between the French of Montreal and the Ojibways of Lake Superior, which brought into the Indians' possession implements of steel, and that bane of the civilized world, " fire-water."

The people had already commenced to inhabit the islands along the river St. Marie, when a quantity of liquor was landed at a point near Grand De Tour, between St. Marie and Mackanaw. The Indians from the upper lakes, as they camped, began to use this liquor quite freely, in order to see its curious effects upon them.

Among these were two families who had lived and hunted the moose together, and had from childhood roamed the wide forest without one word of difference between them.

They also wished to experiment with new drink, which when some drank would cause them to enter into curious antics, others sang war songs, others were jovial, while a few challenged the spectators to combat with their weapons of war.

During this experimenting, the two intimate friends had a quarrel, which resulted in the death of one of them. The murderer seeing what he had done, fled to the woods, to a spot near which they had lived, and there concealed himself. The deed was soon known all over the village. As the murderer had fled, it was agreed by mutual consent and in accordance with their law of retaliation, that the brother of the murderer should be executed in the guilty one's stead. That evening was to be the time of execution, and orders were given that two fires should be built about twenty-five feet apart. A post was placed between the two fires, on which he was to rest himself.

The victim prepared himself by deliberately painting himself with various colors. When the evening came, there were twelve warriors, with bows well strung,

and good arrows, who were to fire at the prisoner.—
The people with eager curiosity looked on. It was
announced that all was ready. The victim walked
calmly from his lodge to the place where he was soon
to represent his brother. The warriors were arranged
at a distance of thirty steps, and the innocent man
stood at the post, where his brother should have stood.

"Don't shoot me till I give you the signal," said he,
as he waved his hand toward heaven. His breast was
painted black, with the exception of a white spot about
the size of a dollar in its centre, which was to be the
point to which the arrows should be aimed.

The warriors and the victim were ready. The fire
blazed, and amid the stillness of the evening, the prisoner was heard singing the death wail :

> " Ne-bah bah-moo-say Ke-zhe-goon-ai,
> Ne ge chog a ye shaw-wod."

Before the last stanza was sung, and as his voice became weak, he turned to the crowd, where he thought
his brother might be lurking, and said—"Ha hay !"—
then continued—"Brother, I am now ready to be killed
in your stead. I will not dishonor the clan I belong to
by endeavoring to shun this fate. If you can endure
the idea that hereafter the Nation will look upon us as
a race of cowards, live ! but I would choose to die in

your stead." As he finished the last lines of the death
song, his brother ran from the woods to his side, and
said—" I am not a coward. I ran to the woods to get
sober, that I might not be killed like a dog. I can soon
be ready, and you shall see how a brave can die." He
then stepped aside, and blackened his breast ; breaking
the ashes, he formed a white spot in the centre of his
breast. Then leaning his back against the post, he began his death song. As its last doleful note died, far
away in the forest glen, he lifted both hands, and bared
his breast to the warriors. Twelve arrows pierced it,
and he fell, the second Indian victim of intemperance.

NOTE.—This traditional story was related to me by
Ne-gah-be-an, in the year 1834, while we camped near
Drumwood's Island on our way up the Sault St. Marie.
It was my purpose some time since to have published a
volume of Indian stories, and trust that I shall be able
to do so in a short time.

CHAPTER X.

" Here are a few of the most unpleasant words
· That ever blotted paper."
SHAKSPEARE.

THE Ojibway language or the language of the Algonquin stock is, perhaps, the most widely spoken of any
in North America. The Atlantic tribes partook of this
idiom when they were first discovered.

The snows of the North bounded the people who
spoke this language on that side, while in the South as
far as the Potomac and the mountains of Virginia, down
the Ohio, over the plains of Illinois to the East of the
upper waters of the Father of Rivers, Nations resided
three or four hundred years ago who could speak so as
to be understood by each other. A person might have
travelled nearly one thousand miles from the head of
Lake Superior, and yet not journey from the sound of
this dialect.

In consequence of this universality of their language, the Nation has had a wide-spreading influence. Many of the Nation have travelled from the main body to other lands : thus passing in contact with other Nations they have adopted their customs, and have so intermixed the two languages, that the original Ojibway is not now so generally spoken, within a thousand miles of the Ojibway or Great Lake, as formerly.

Mr. H. R. Schoolcraft, who has studied the language more than any other person, and to some purpose, has often said through the press as well in private conversation, that there is in it that which few other languages possess ; a force of expression, with music in its words and poetry in their meaning. I cannot express fully the beauty of the language, I can only refer to those who have studied it as well as other languages, and quote their own writing in saying, " every word has its appropriate meaning, and with additional syllables give additional force to the meaning of most words." After reading the English language, I have found words in the Indian combining more expressiveness. There are many Indian words which when translated into English lose their force, and do not convey so much meaning in one sentence as the original does in one word.

It would require an almost infinitude of English words

to describe a thunder-storm, and after all you would have but a feeble idea of it. In the Ojibway language, we say "*Be-wah-sam-moog.*" In this we convey the idea of a continual glare of lightning, noise, confusion—an awful whirl of clouds, and much more. Observe the smoothness of its words :—

Ah-nung-o-kah,	The starry heavens.
Bah-bah-me-tum,	Obedience.
Che-baum,	Soul.
De goo wah skah,	The rippling wave.
E nah-kay-yah,	The way.
Gah-gah-geeh,	Raven.
How-wah-do-seh,	Stone carrier (fish.)
Ish peming,	Heaven.
Jeen quon,	Earthquake.
Kah-ke-nah,	All.
Mah-nah-ta-nis,	Sheep.
Nah-nah-gum-moo,	Singing.
O-nah-ne quod,	Pleasant weather.
Pah-pah-say,	Woodpecker.
Quah-nauge,	Pretty.
Sah-se-je-won,	Rapids.
Tah-que-shin,	He or she comes.
Wah-be-goo-ne,	Lily.
Yah-no-tum,	Unbelief.
Ze-bee-won,	Streams.

Upon examination it will be found that there are several letters not sounded, to wit : F, L, R, V, X, though
Carver mentions in his vocabulary the use of the letter
L in several instances. This no doubt he did because
he lacked a perfect understanding of the language. The
same may be said of the letter R. We have none of
the mouthing as of the thick sound of the letter L, nor
any of the gutteral accompaniments of the letter R. To
the contrary, all the softness of the vowels are sounded
without many of the harsh notes of the consonants, and
this produces that musical flow of words for which the
language is distinguished.

It is a natural language. The pronunciation of the
names of animals, birds and trees are the very sounds
these produce ; for instance; Hoot Owl, *O-o-me-seh ;*
Owl, *Koo-koo-ko-ooh ;* River, *See-be ;* Rapids, *Sah se-je-*
won. "*See*" is the sound of the waters on the rocks.—
"*Sah-se*" the commotion of waters, and from its sound
occurs its name.

The softness of the language is caused, as I have before said, by the peculiar sounding of all the vowels ;
though there is but little poetic precision in the formation of verse, owing to the want of a fine discriminating
taste by those who speak it.

A language, derived, as this is, from the peculiarities

of the country in which it is spoken, must, necessarily, partake of its nature. Our orators have filled the forest with the music of their voices, loud as the roar of a waterfall, yet soft and wooing as the gentle murmur of a mountain stream. We have had warriors who have stood on the banks of lakes and rivers, and addressed with words of irresistible and persuasive eloquence their companions in arms.

The Ojibway language has not yet been reduced to a perfect written form. An attempt to do this was made by the lamented Summerfield, who in his degree of usefulness would not have dishonored his name had he lived. Close study was followed by a consumptive disease, which terminated his life before his contemplated work was finished. In his attempt he followed too much the English idiom in forming a grammar of the Ojibway language.

The records of the Ojibways have a two-fold meaning ; the hieroglyphic symbols of material objects represent the transmission of a tradition from one generation to another. This refers more particularly to their religion, which is itself founded on tradition. Picture writing is most prevalent, and is used altogether in their medicine and hunting songs. Here are figures which suggest sentences to be sung :

This is one of their war sons, which might read in English thus :

I.

I will haste to the land of the foe,

With warriors clad with the bow.

II.

I will drink the blood of their very heart ;

I will change their joy into sorrow's smart

Their braves, their sires will I defy,

And a Nation's vengeance satisfy.

III.

They are in their homes, now happy and free ;

No frowning cloud o'er their camp they see ;

Yet the youngest of mine shall see the tall

Braves, scattered, wandering, and fall.

The warrior is represented by the figure of a man with a bow about him, and arrows in his hand ; with the plume of the eagle waving over his head, indicative of his acquaintance with war life. The next figure represents a watching warrior, equally brave, but the heart is represented as dead. The curve of his mouth shows that he is shouting. The next figure represents a person with long hair, an indication that the best of the enemy's warriors were to fall, and their wail must be heard like the wail of a woman. The wigwam with its smoke curling upwards, indicates a council fire and the defiance of an attack. The other wigwams are seen without fire ; and the black one signifies silence and death.

When I was young I was taught this, and while singing I could, in imagination, see the enemy, though none were within a hundred miles.

In their war songs animals are likewise represented in various attitudes. A rattle is made of deer's hoofs which is shook during the singing.

This rattle was sometimes used for the purpose of transmitting news from one nation to another ; but in most cases shells were used for this purpose. I have been present in Canada when a string of beads has been received from the head waters of Lake Superior. A profound silence ensued, then followed a revelation of the message, and at its close a prolonged grunting sound from the vast assembly signified the people's assent.

There is a place where the sacred records are deposited in the Indian country. These records are made on one side of bark and board plates, and are examined once in fifteen years, at which time the decaying ones are replaced by new plates.

This secrecy is not generally known by those people who have searched with interest the Indian, and traced him in all his wanderings to get an idea of his religion and his worship, which however absurd they may have seemed, have nevertheless been held in so rigid respect that he has formed for it a cloak of almost impenetrable mystery. He concluded that all Nature around him was clothed in mystery—that innumerable spirits were ever near to forward a good object and retard a bad one, and that they existed as a chain connecting heaven with earth. His medicine bag contained all those native things of the forest around which, in his opinion, the greatest mystery gathered ; as the more of mystery, the more of the Great Spirit seemed to be attached to them. A whale was an object of much importance, because it was dedicated to the Supreme Being, and to approach it, or look upon it irreverently, would offend him and his children. They therefore never drew near it but with the most profound silence and veneration. With this great awe of spiritual things in his mind, he feels reluctant to reveal all that he knows of his worship and the objects and rites which perpetuate it.

Most Indian Nations of the West have places in which they deposit the records which are said to have originated their worship. The Ojibways have three such de-

positories near the waters of Lake Superior. Ten of the
wisest and most venerable of the Nation dwell near
these, and are appointed guardians over them.

Fifteen years intervene between each opening. At
the end of this time, if any vacancies have been caused
by death, others are chosen in the spring of the year,
who, about the month of August, are called to witness
the opening of the depositories. As they are being
opened, all the information known respecting them is
given to the new members; then the articles are placed
before them. After this, the plates are closely examined, and if any have begun to decay they are taken out;
an exact fac simile is made and placed in its stead.—
The old one is divided equally among the wise men. It
is very highly valued for having been deposited; as a
sacred article, every fibre of it is considered sacred, and
whoever uses it may be made wise. It is considered
efficacious for any good purpose it may be put.

These records are written on slate rock, copper, lead,
and on the bark of birch trees. The record is said to
be a transcript of what the Great Spirit gave to the Indian after the flood, and by the hands of wise men has
been transmitted to other parts of the country ever since.
Here is a code of moral laws which the Indian calls
"a path made by the Great Spirit." They believe that

a long and prosperous life will be the result of obeying that law. The records contain certain emblems which transmit the ancient form of worship, and the rules for the dedication of four priests who alone are to expound them. In them is represented how man lived happy in his wigwam, before death was in the world, and the path he then followed marked out an example for those of the present time.

During my travels over the whole extent of the Nation, I have been informed of a great many facts respecting these sacred depositories of which most of my brethren are ignorant.

The Chief of Lac Coart, Oreille, ("Moose Tail,") in the spring of 1836, related to my uncle John Taunchey, of Rice Lake, C. W., an account of one of these depositories near the mouth of "Round Lake."

He said he had been chosen as one of the guardians about five years previous, and that the guardians had for a long time selected as the places of deposit the most unsuspected spot, where they dug fifteen feet, and sunk large cedar trees around the excavation. In the centre was placed a large hollow cedar log, besmeared at one end with gum. The open end is uppermost, and in it are placed the records, after being enveloped in the down of geese or swan, which are changed at each examination. These feathers are afterwards used in war, being supposed to have a protective power. When camping, a few of these feathers are left near each place where the warriors dance.

These are some of the figures used by us in writing. With these, and from others of a similar class, the Ojibways can write their war and hunting songs.

An Indian well versed in these can send a communication to another Indian, and by them make himself as well understood as a pale face can by letter.

There are over two hundred figures in general use for all the purposes of correspondence. Material things are represented by pictures of them.

THE CHARACTERS USED IN PICTURE WRITING.

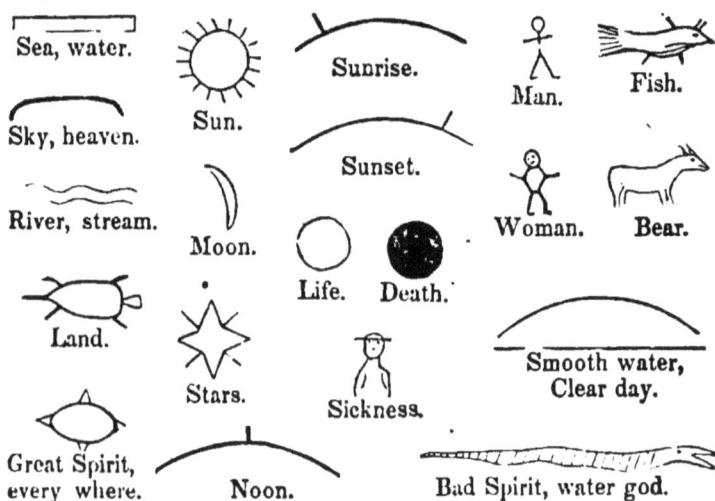

Sea, water.

Sky, heaven.

River, stream.

Land.

Great Spirit, every where.

Sun.

Moon.

Stars.

Noon.

Sunrise.

Sunset.

Life. Death.

Sickness.

Man.

Woman.

Bad Spirit, water god.

Fish.

Bear.

Smooth water, Clear day.

Rain, cloudy.

Old tree.   Tree.   Spirit.

Deer, Moose.

Duck, water birds.

Islands.

Bad spring under earth.

Storm, windy.

Hemlock.

Medicine Lodge.

War.   Trees, woods.   Bad.   Wounded water god.

Bad Spirit, Medicine.   Worship, Medicine, pure.   Scalps, number.   Young warrior.

Night.   Fight-Man, Bad Spirit.   Mountains.

Spirits above.   Great.   Sea Monster eat man.

Animals under ground.   Spirits under water.   Cold, snow.

Fire.   Ran.   Walked, passed.   Hand, did so.   Bear Killed

Dream.   See.   Speak.   Stand.

Invitations to Indians to come and worship in the spring are made in the following form :—

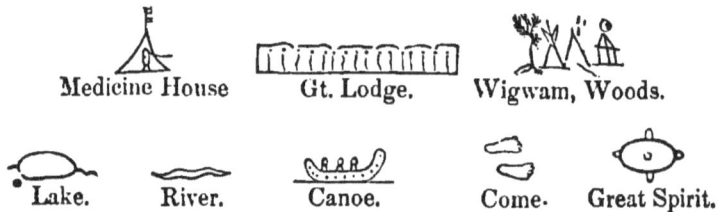

Medicine House.   Gt. Lodge.   Wigwam, Woods.

Lake.   River.   Canoe.   Come.   Great Spirit.

The whole story would thus read :—

" Hark to the words of the Sa-ge-mah."

" The Great Medicine Lodge will be ready in eight days."

" Ye who live in the woods and near the Lakes and by streams of water, come with your canoes or by land to the worship of the Great Spirit."

In the above, the wigwam and the medicine pale or worship, represent the depositories of medicine, record and work. The Lodge is represented with men in it ; the dots above indicate the number of days.

These picture representations were used by the Ojibways until the introduction of European manners among them. When this occurred, they neglected in a great degree their correspondence with other nations, except by special messengers, and became very cautious in giving information respecting their religious worship to the whites, because they, the whites, ridiculed it. It is

worthy of remark in this place, that however ridiculous
the simple rites and ceremonies by which the untutored
Indian showed his faith in the Great Spirit may have
appeared, they were dear and sacred to him, and ridicule should never have been used to disabuse his mind
of his long formed opinions. It was a fruitless way to
reclaim him, by the attempt to do so by ridicule ; and
man could never by such means imbue his mind with
the principles of true worship.

In times of danger or in the progress of a war, beads
and shells were used for the purpose of conveying a
message, and this custom is yet in vogue.

These beads and shells were colored, and each had a
meaning, according to its place on the string. *Black*
indicated war or death— *White*, peace and prosperity—
Red, the heart of the enemy would represent—*Partial
white* or *red,* or both intermixed, the beginning of peace
or the commencement of war.

Numerals are marked on the shell. The knot gives
information of its starting point, or the name of the person sending it. In stringing the shells or beads, the
end of the sentence is strung first, so that the first word
of the message is in the person's hand. This manner
of correspondence is the most common.

Three hundred years ago the Delawares sent com-

munications in this way to the Shawnees in Sandusky
Lake Erie; and they to the Ojibways in Superior and
Huron.

This mode was practised by Pontiac in his appeals
to the Indians of Michigan, Huron, and the prairies of
the West, during the wars. The Indians say that these
beads cannot give false stories, for it is not possible for
the man who takes it to alter or add to them, during
his journey.

CHAPTER XI.

THEIR GOVERNMENT.

" Each state must have its pallaces ;
Kingdoms have edjcts ; cities have their charters ;
Even the wild outlaw in his forest walk
Keeps yet some touch of civil discipline."

POPE.

THE rulers of the Ojibways were inheritors of the power they held. However, when a new country was conquered or new dominions annexed, the first rulers were elected to their offices. Afterwards the descendants of these elected chiefs ruled the Nation, or tribe, and thus the power became hereditary. On the death of the chief ruler, should the son be under age, the brother of the deceased rules in his stead, until the youth becomes a man, when after the display of much ceremony, he takes his seat at the head of the Council of the Nation. •

These young rulers are apt to be more cautious in the

exercise of their governing power than those who possess more mature age with its more mature vanities.—
Having been trained, and trained well by the aged wise
men, they enter upon their duties conscious of their responsibilities, and remembering the advise they have
received from their elders.

Councils were only convened by the Chiefs who presided on important occasions.   Those who sat at these
councils, did so according to their age and wisdom.—
Among these a free discussion was allowed, the youngest
generally remaining silent listeners to the wisdom of
the aged.

A Chief had always two braves at his side—one was
always near him day and night.   Their duties were
various.   At times watching the lodge of the Chief—at
others, sent on important errands for the Nations.   They
were frequently ordered not to stand still on their way,
or sit down to rest until they had delivered their message and received an answer.

Being commanded to go on one of these errands, the
young brave utters " hah," signifying his assent to do
all that is required of him.   He then takes the brace of
beads, turns suddenly about and proceeds on his way·

Day after day, night after night, he journeys on till he
reaches his destination and does the command of his Chief.

I knew a young man by the name of John Loper. He was the best runner my father had, and was a man of great energy and activity. He travelled with us when we removed to the north towards the Ottawa River.

In the dead of winter the track of his snow shoes might have been seen far and near.

In the spring of the year we often sat together in the open woods, he relating his adventures and I listening to his account of having crossed swollen streams on cakes of ice or logs of wood, holding fast to his only hope of life with his clothes all in rags, and his body so torn and bruised by the brush-wood and briars, that his moccasins were filled with blood.

John died in 1839, much lamented. Since then the Ojibways have not seen a man possessing so much energy or one so determined upon surmounting all obstacles that lie in his path as he was.

This person acted the part of a commissary when any thing was to be divided in the village. Formerly they received nothing for such services, but now they receive a stated salary and a provision for their expenses. They traverse the Ojibway country in all directions, and during the winter inform the people that they must meet together at the first change of the " flower moon" (May)

at the place named by the Chief. All matters of importance are decided by the Chief. He pronounces all
marriages, and his word settles all difficulties of every
name and nature. No appeal can be made from his
decisions, as he is the highest.

Any one found guilty of a misdemeanor is brought
before the Chief, who reprimands him before the crowd.

When a murder is committed, the Chief can act as he
pleases in regard to the offender, but should he not in-
terfere, the relations of the deceased take the law in
their own hands, and execute death upon the murderer.

Those who murder never attempt to run away or con-
ceal their guilt, but repair to their wigwam. If the
Chief learns that the crime was provoked, he shields and
protects the criminal : if not, he is put to death. His
life is at every moment in danger should he live.

Theft is punished by making the thief publicly known
and being clothed as such. In this way adultery is punished in the case of a man : in that of a woman, she has
her hair cut from ear to ear, which is a mark of disgrace.
It does not devolve upon any Chief in particular to make
or form a war party, but any of the braves can muster
together a band of volunteers. Those who have a
desire to do so, can join these parties, the number of
each party being regulated entirely according to the

bravery of the individual who forms it. Among the
Indians there have been no written laws. Customs
handed down from generation to generation have
been the only laws to guide them. Every one might
act different from what was considered right did he
choose to do so, but such acts would bring upon him
the censure of the Nation, which he dreaded more than
any corporal punishment that could be inflicted upon him.

This fear of the Nation's censure acted as a mighty
band, binding all in one social, honorable compact. They
would not as brutes be whipped into duty. They would
as men be persuaded to the right.

Of late years, law has borne with it very many evils.
We can judge somewhat of the character of a community
by its buildings. Prisons, penitentiaries, and poor-
houses are bad signs.

Before law was introduced, the Indians had none of
these. Whatever we had was shared alike. In times
of gladness all partook of the joy; and when suffering
came all alike suffered.

I believe communities can be governed by the pure
rules of christianity, with less coercion than the laws of
civilized nations, at present, impose upon their subjects.

This however cannot be done unless each is resolved
upon a manly forbearance of those minor evils which in

all cases precede great ones.   A vast amount of evidence
can be adduced to prove that force has tended to bru-
talize rather than ennoble the Indian race.   The more
a man is treated as a brother, the less demand for law.
The less law there is, the more will man be honored
thus.

One of the most favorable indications in the Algonquin tribes of their ultimate adoption of a pure christianity is the simplicity of their government, and of their
life and manners.   To this the eye of the missionary
should be directed, and all his actions be conformed to
this happy state of affairs.

Of late, the General Councils of the Christian Ojibways
have been convened and carried on in the same manner
as the public meetings of the whites are conducted.

The last General Council, which consisted of Ojibways
and Ottawas, was held at Sangeeng.   The Chiefs came
from St. Clair, Huron, Ontario, Simcoe, Rice, and Mud
Lakes.

The object of this convention was to devise plans by
which the tract of land then held by the Sangeeng Indians, could be held for the sole use of the Ojibway
Nation ; to petition the government for aid in establish-
ing a Manual Labor School ; to ascertain the views and
feelings of the Chiefs in relation to forming one large set-

tlement among themselves at Owen's Sound, where they might live in future, and to attend to other things of minor importance.

There were forty-eight Chiefs present from Canada West alone. Chief Sawyer took the chair, and the writer had the honor of being *Vice President.* Chief John Jones of Owen Sound, was appointed to deliver the opening address, in which he was to give an outline of the subjects to be discussed.

The meeting was called to order ; and after singing and prayer, the former by the members of the council, the latter by Chief Sunday, in which all united, Chief Jones arose. After casting a piercing glance over the assembly, he spoke as follows :—

" Brothers ! You have been called from all parts of Canada, and even from the North of Georgia Bay.

You are from your homes, your wives and your children.

We might regret this separation were it not for the circumstances that call you here.

Fellow Chiefs and Brothers ! I have pondered with deep solicitude our present condition ; and the future welfare of our children as well as of ourselves. I have studied deeply and anxiously in order to arrive at a true knowledge of the proper course to be pursued in order to secure to us and our descendants, and even to others around us, the greatest amount of peace, health, happiness and usefulness.   The interests of the Ojibways are near and dear to my heart; for them I have passed many a sleepless night, and have oftentimes been wearied with an agitated mind.

The people of these Nations, I am proud to say, are my brethren ; many of them are bone of my bone ; and for them, if needs be, I could willingly, yea cheerfully sacrifice my life.

Brothers, you see my heart.*   Fellow Chiefs and Warriors !   I have looked over your wigwams through Canada, and have arrived at the conclusion, that you are in a warm place : your neighbors, the whites, are kindling fires all around you.†   One purpose for which we have been called together, is to devise some plan by which we can live together ; and become a happy people, so that our fires may not go out (Nation become extinct) but may be kindled in one place, which will prove a blessing to our children.

Brothers !   Some of you are living on small parcels of

* Here the speaker held out a piece of white paper, emblematic of a pure heart.

† Reference was here made to the clearing of the lands—The trees being burnt for that purpose.

land, and others on Islands. We now offer you any portion of the land which we own in this region ; that we may during the remainder of our days, smoke the pipe of friendship; live and die together, and see our children reared on one spot and join there in their youthful sports. We ask no more from you. We feel for you. We feel for your children's sake, and therefore we make this proposition.

Brothers ! There are many subjects worthy of your consideration, but the most important are

1st. Whether it would be better for the whole Ojibway Nation to reside on this, our own territory ?

2nd. Would it not be well to devise ways and means for the establishment and support of Manual Labor Schools, for the benefit of the nation ?

3d. Ought a petition to be drawn up and be presented to our Great Father, (Governor General) for the purpose of fixing upon a definite time for the distribution of the annual " presents" and the small annuities of each tribe ?

4th. Is it desirable to petition our Great Father to appoint a resident Indian Interpreter, to assist the agent at Toronto ?

5th. As we (the Christian part of the Nation) have abandoned our former customs and ceremonies, ought

we not to make our own laws, in order to give character and stability to our Chiefs, as well as to empower
them to treat with the Government under which we live,
that they may, from time to time, present all our grievances, and other matters to it?   .

My Chiefs, Brothers, Warriors! This morning, (pointing upwards) look up and see the blue sky; there are
no clouds; the Great Spirit is smiling upon us. May
he preside over us, that we may make a long, smooth and
straight path for our children.   ·

It is true, I seldom see you all; but this morning I
shake hands with you all in my heart.

Brothers! This is all I have to say."

On taking his seat eighty-four Chiefs responded "*Hah*"!
an exclamation of great applause.

Several Chiefs addressed the Council, highly appro-
ving of the plans proposed, and expressing their gratitude for the liberal offer of lands

THE APPROACH OF CIVILIZATION.

CHAPTER XII.

" The generous Author of the Universe,
Who reins the winds, gives the vast ocean bounds,
And circumscribes the floating world their rounds."

" Sees God in clouds or hears Him in the wind."

THE Ojibway Nation believed in a Great Good Spirit, and in a Bad Spirit. They had also " gods innumerable," among which was " the god of war," " the god of hunting," and " the god of the fowls of the air."

The skies were filled with the deities they worshipped, and the whole forest awakened with their whispers. The lakes and streams were the places of their resort, and mountains and vallies alike their abode. All the remarkable spots in the country were considered their favorite resorts. These were the peaks of rocky cliffs ; the clefts of craggy mounts. Water-falls were thought to be their sporting scenes.

J

The sky was the home of the god who held a watchful care over every star. They heard him whisper in the gentle breeze, or howl in the tempest. He had dominion over all the three heavens, and sometimes amused himself by hurling stars from their stations and causing them on their passage to the earth to change into demons to wrong and perplex the people who inhabited the place of their destination.

The constellations of stars were council gatherings of the god. The brightest were ruling spirits, appointed by the Great Spirit as guardians of the lesser ones. Clusters of stars were the populous cities of the celestials.

In the stories of the wigwam, mention is made of some of these high born personages coming to earth to dwell among the people ; also of men going up and becoming inhabitants of the skies. They say animals have received wings ; and some of them from heaven.

Were all the stories that are related of the skies written, it would be found that each star has connected with it some strange event. The history of the tradition of the stars, according to Indian tradition, would be a history indeed, and would rank among the " curiosities of literature."

The earth teemed with all sorts of spirits, good and bad, those of the forest clothed themselves with moss.

During a shower of rain, thousands of them are shelter-
ed in a flower.

The Ojibway, as he reclines beneath the shade of his
forest trees, imagines these gods to be about him. He
detects their tiny voices in the insect's hum. With half
closed eyes he beholds them sporting by thousands on
a sunray. In the evening they are seen and heard

> " Above, below, on every side,
> Their little minium forms displayed
> In all the tricksy pomp of fairy pride."

They have a special god presiding over the most
noted herbs of the earth. These are subject to this being who is called the god of Medicine Men or women
are deemed capable of learning the virtues of roots from
him, and often fast in order to gain his favor. In time
of war they carry certain roots with them, which according to their idea, prevent the balls of an enemy from
striking them.

The Ojibways place much dependence upon dreams.
They are to them the omens of good or bad fortune.—
Fastings of considerable length are endured in order to
win the good will of the god. These fasts are at various times. The summer season is the time of the children's fasting. I well remember the tedious fast of four
or five days I underwent when quite young, and what

a tremendous appetite I had when it was over; as fai exceeding that of the renowned Gogerins, as theirs did that of the Eastmans.

I cannot better portray the influence of dreams upon the Indian's mind than by relating a story of an Indian damsel, who according to the custom of fasting, determined to do so in a remarkable romantic spot, near Grand Island. A cave in each side of this cove is to be seen at the present day, with a rivulet coming down to the edge of the lake. A rock arches the stream similar to the natural bridge of Virginia; on the tops of which is a pine tree standing alone. In one of the caves lies a ledge of rock, and it was to this the maiden resorted to ask the favor of the gods.

In a summer season she with her friends were coasting along the southern shore, camping every evening. Suddenly, as it were, she became pensive. She said but little, and her parents wondered, not knowing the cause of her change. Her mother thought she had become angered, and inquired of her whether such was the fact. She merely smiled and said Kah ween.

Evening after evening passed, and on each she took her accustomed stroll along the beach, picking up Cornelian stones, which are found there in great numbers. one evening she was seen standing on the peak of the pictured rocks ; and as the sun was passing the horizon, and the waves dashed furiously, she was heard to sing for the first time. Her long black hair floated upon the wind, and her voice was heard above the rustling of the leaves and the noise of the waters. When night came, she could not be seen. She had fled to the rocky cave, from whence were to go up her petitions to the gods.

The people lighted their birch torches, and wandered over the forest, but they could not observe the slightest sign of the maiden's presence. They were obliged to wait until the morning. At length day dawned,—the sun gradually arose. Her parents and the people went in search of her; they looked in every place—in woodland, in glades, upon the shore and in the caves of the rocks, yet could not find her. Day passed. Night came. They called her by name, "*Shah-won-o-equa*," (Lady of the South) but she answered not, and they were left in great distress, conjecturing about her situation. The next day was spent in like manner, but with no better success. As evening approached, they thought they heard her voice. They all listened. " Yes," said the father, " it is Shah-won-o-equa." The voice seemed to be at so great a distance among the rocks that they could not reach the spot from which it proceeded before night came, and the voice departed.

Anxiously they awaited the approach of day, and when it came, with all possible speed they hasted in the direction in which they had heard the voice. Not seeing any path made by her footsteps, they concluded that it was not her voice, but that of a spirit they had heard, and that she had been taken away by the Great Spirit whose track* was seen on the rocks.

The next night when the sun was sinking, they again heard the voice, sounding as if on the cliffs of the rocks. They looked, when they beheld standing on a lofty peak the lost maiden, gazing at the departing sun, and chanting her evening prayer to the gods of her fathers. The parents were convinced that the form they beheld could not be a spirit, but in reality their daughter. The next morning another search was made, which resulted in finding her sitting in the cave, having robes of fur covering her head, and boughs of cedar all around her. Since the day she left her home, she had taken no food, and though a rivulet of pure water coursed along at her feet, she touched it not.

She was asked why she had not informed her friends of her situation. She replied, that she wanted to fast, and that to do so, it was best for her to remain there in

---

* The marks on the pictured rocks are thought to be the footsteps of the Great Spirit.

seclusion. Her mother wished her to go with her to their wigwam, but the girl refused to do so, until the gods were propitious to her.

The following day her mother again visited her, and inquired whether the gods had visited her since their last interview. She replied that they had not, but that she was resolved upon remaining there until they did. She then covered her head with furs and laid down.

In the cave, on the ledge of rocks, she waited to receive the god of war, the god of the vegetable kingdom, and the god of the waters, whom she expected would visit her in her dreams, or in a visible form, and converse with her.

That evening the waves roared furiously, and the winds moaned. She fell asleep. She saw a young warrior approach, who standing over her, gazed at her as her raven hair was tossed about by the wind. Bending over her, he said :—

" Equa ! (woman) I have watched thee these three days—and now I come to speak to you. What will you have ? The furs from the woods—the plumes of rare birds—the animals of the forest—or a knowledge of the properties of the wild flowers?"

" Young man !" said she, " I know thy fathers are the unseen spirits of the earth. I want not the furs,

nor the plumes, nor the animals.   I want a knowledge
of the roots that I may relieve the Nation's sufferings,
and prolong the lives of the aged who live among us."

"And is this for what you have fasted so long and so
faithfully ?"

" Yes—the woods had their charms for me when I
was small, but now the long wail of my people over
their accumulating woes sounds in my ears.   The forest
yields pleasant fruits, and the lake shores are decorated
with pebbles of various hues.   I loved to gather the
lilies and the flowers, till I learned there was life in
them and a power to impart it.   Then I hasted to this
secluded spot, and, that I might learn the secret of the
herbs and flowers, I have fasted here in seclusion, waiting the approach of thy fathers to teach them to me."   .

" Then wait for them," said the young man, "for they
will soon come."

He left.   Night came on—dark night, and she dream-
ed that she was placed on the edge of a high rock which
was suspended over the great prairies of the West, and
that before her many Nations assembled to join in a
great ball play.

She stood watching the progress of the game, and
observed that the women were the fleetest, and that one
of them actually won the prize.

The stranger again stood at the damsel's side.—
" There," said he, " do you see that maiden among the
crowd?" She answered that she did. " So will your
Nation look to you, when an assembled multitude
gather to join in the Nation's ball play. If this will
satisfy you, go now, return to your mother."

He left her again, and in much agitation she awoke
from her eventful sleep.

The morning dawned, when again her mother inquired whether she had been visited by the gods. She
made no reply. Her mother left, but soon again returned and without success importuned her to leave
the cave.

That night the winds were fierce, and the waters
dashed with great power against the pictured rocks.—
The earth trembled as the thunder growled above it,
and the frequent, almost continuous lightning caused the
streams of water to appear like floods of molten gold.

Notwithstanding the tumult of nature, the maiden
fell asleep. Numerous individuals surrounded her.—
One was clad in scarlet—another in blue—another in
black, and another in white cloth. They sang a song,
then left, with the exception of one, who it appeared remained to reveal to her the purport of what she saw.
He was old and quite bald-headed.

"No-sis!" (child) said he, "do you know those who came and sung to you?" She replied that she did not. "Why," continued he, "they are all my children—they are the birds you see in the forests—they will always sing for you."

"And I am their parent," said a great Bald Eagle, adjusting his wings, and suddenly starting off.

The next morning, these same birds came and sang near her head, while she was musing over her pleasant dream.

The Red-breast Robin, the Scarlet birds, the Blue Jays, and the tiny Humming-birds, were about her.— She thought the gods had been propitious to her, and her heart filled with emotions of gratitude.

When the next morning came, she began to find her strength fast failing. Her mother again came with her usual entreaties, but to them all she remained silent, and apparently did not notice her or them.

She had a number of remarkable dreams. In one of these she saw two beings who came to conduct her to a hill, from whence she could see the plains below. In climbing the hill, they ascended many steeps, and as she stood on the summit of one of these, her attendants bade her look back and see what had been passed.

She turned. What a sight! The clouds rolled beneath her ; above all was clear. She saw the path she had followed, and around it she beheld the lightning's flash.

"'That which is before you, bordering on the great hill, is Infancy. It is pleasant, but dangerous. The rocks represent the perilous times of life. But keep moving: look not behind you again, until you have reached the highest peak."

Up—up they went. The way was diversified—sometimes safe, at other times dangerous. When they had fully ascended, they beheld on one side the deep, broad ocean : at the other, the lofty, numerous mountains of the West—Ocean glittering in the sunlight—Nature rearing its battlements to the skies.

One of the maiden's companions touched her head, when one-half of her hair was changed to snowy whiteness. Then she awoke, much exhausted.

The next morning, when her mother came, and, as before, wished her to accompany her, she determined that if on her next visit she should refuse, she would take her from the cave by main force.

In her last dream she saw a canoe sailing upon Lake Superior. It came to where she stood, and she was asked to enter it. She did so, when one of her visiters began to chant a song :—

"Ba bah mah she yon nee beeng gay,
Ba bah moo say ah keeng gay."

" I walk on the waves of the sea,
I travel o'er hill and dale."

They proceeded in the canoe till they were far from the sight of land, and the waters around them were unmoved.

"When becalmed," said they, " sing this, and you will hear us whisper to you. They then returned her to the shore.

When she awoke, the storm was yet raging, and the voices of the gods were heard in the winds among the trees. Believing she had gained the good will of the spirits she had retired to meet, she permitted herself, when her mother came, to be taken to the wigwam.— It was the tenth day of her fasting, and her strength was nearly gone.

" By my fasting I have received the favor of the gods," said she to the friends who crowded around her. " I have travelled the journey of life, and have learned that I shall not die until half of my hair has turned white."

Since that time, I have seen that girl but once. In the year 1842, while sailing along Lake Superior, on its southern shore, I came rather unexpectedly to a cluster of wigwams, where I saw Shah-won a-qua, and listened with deep interest to her relation of the dreams of her childhood. I gave her a few wild ducks from my boat load of game, and a yard of scarlet cloth—a fabric which is esteemed very highly by the Indian women. This I did in payment for those early impressions she had made upon my mind, leading me to believe that the noble deeds of man are those, and those only, which are performed for the good of others; and that virtue will be alike rewarded in the future, whether it be found and cherished in pagan lands or in Christian temples.

There is one Ruler whom we call *Ke-sha-mon-e-doo*, "Benevolent Spirit," or *Ke-che-mon-e-doo*, "Great Spirit." This being is over the universe at the same time, ruling all under different names, such as "the god of war," " the god of the fish," &c.

The Sun is the wigwam of the Great Spirit, and it is as the abode of this being that the Indians view that luminary. Very few of the Northern Indians ever held the idea that the Sun was an object of worship.

When great Councils are held, or the Medicine worship is in progress, if the day is clear the Indians think that the Great Spirit smiles upon them. If it be cloudy, it is thought the Great Spirit is displeased.

None of the Indian youth are allowed to speak the

name of the Great Spirit without proper marks of veneration. There was a time when they did not take the
name of God in vain, but this habit some have acquired
since being civilized (!) The rigid, though not too rigid
rules they have adopted, might have been sustained had
not evil entered with the good during their intercourse
with the whites. As it is, there are children who, as
soon as their tongues get in shape, use them to blas-
pheme their Creator. I never heard a man swear without its causing my blood to run cold. Why, pale face,
let me tell you, the Bad Spirit is a saint to such a man.

That worship of the Indians called "Me-day Worship," is conducted as follows :

When a lodge is made, its length is in proportion to
the number of persons who are to occupy it. Its width
is generally from twenty paces. Long poles are placed
in the ground which meet at their tops to within about
two feet of each other. Over these awning, or roof is
formed. In the centre of the lodge is a pole, which we
call a meeting pole, or *Me-day Wahtich.* It has painted on it a representation of the Great Spirit. The sides
of the lodge are covered with boughs or mats. The
great medicine drum is beat for three days and nights
previous to the time of worship. Those who have
received their lectures for a year or more are

brought and placed in the centre. The priest or chief medicine man, with powder in his hand, sings at one end of the lodge, a song. This concluded, he goes to the other side and repeats it. They then aim a blow at their student, who falls to the ground as though fainting, as well he might after such a lesson. The *professor* sings again : after which a spot is made in the centre of the subject's breast, where it is supposed the medicine shell entered. This shell, which the teacher is said to blow from himself to his student, and which he is told will remain with him during life, we call, *Me-day-me-gis* (shell).

In a short time the initiated are made to kneel before the Medicine Bag, which is held as sacred. Then a person comes near the kneeling man and opens a belt of wampum, or shells, from which he takes the line, an emblem of life ; one is crooked, the other straight. The various articles to be used are then opened and all explained.

During the two days preceding this worship, great preparations are made. Children dress ; old and young are fantastically decorated with feathers, paints, and the skin of wild beasts.

The privilege of joining in this worship is granted by the elder members. Some children are allowed to do

ιο, though very young. When any are very sick, the
elders hold a consultation and propose that the sick
person be initiated, as it is thought in this way they will
receive the favor of the Great Spirit, and get better.—
Generally, however, lectures are given for one or two
years to the candidates for initiation, in which they are
taught the responsibilities they are to assume.

I believe this "Me-day Worship" is common among
most of the Indian tribes in the West and North. It
resembles in some particulars the secret societies, so
called in the United States. Members of different tribes
when they meet are admitted to the lodge, on their
knowledge of it, even though their ignorance of the language of each other, renders it necessary to use signs in
making it known.

While the Medicine Worship is progressing, a little
lodge is made near the other, where the chief man has
in keeping all their medicine bags, songs, and emblem.
In this lodge the preparatory lectures are given, as also
when the initiation is over, the initiated is accepted with
the songs they have learned. None of the uninitiated
are allowed in it.

Some years ago, a gentleman travelling in the Sioux
Village, below St. Paul, was told by a waggish Indian
to go in there and smoke with the old man. Sure

enough, in he went, and as soon as he was seated, the
tug of war came. One pulled his hat off; another
pushed him out of the lodge, and when he asked for
his hat, he found they had pushed that out in advance
of him. Somewhat resolved upon having his own way,
he again went in, or attempted to do so, when he was
met at the entrance, thrown down, and in the scramble
for his life and hat, surrendered the tail of his coat to
an Indian lad, who very adroitly cut it off. He could
not comprehend the meaning of such treatment until I
explained it to him. He thought them rude. I thought
so too—but he laughed over it, and finally turned it off
by saying—" 'twas a good joke "—of which he was often reminded when he examined the fit of his coat or
the fur of his hat.

The origin of the Indian's belief in this Medicine
Worship is to be found in the following traditional story, which is usually related to any one when about to
join the clan. I received it myself upon passing the
mysterious ordeal.

When Keshamonedoo made the red men, he made
them happy. The men were larger, were fleeter on
foot, were more dexterous in games, and lived to an
older age than now.

The forest abounded with game, the trees were load-
K

ed with fruit, and birds who have now a black plumage were dressed with pure white. The birds and the fowls ate no flesh, for the wide prairies were covered with fruits and vegetables. The fish in the waters were large. The Monedoo from heaven watched the blaze of the wigwams' fires, and these were as countless as the stars in the sky.

Strange visitants from heaven descended every few days, and inquired of the Indians whether any thing was wrong. Finding them happy and contented, they returned to their high homes.

These were tutelar gods, and they consulted with the sages of the different villages, and advised all not to climb a vine which grew on the earth, and whose top reached the sky, as it was the ladder on which the spirits descended from heaven to earth, to bless the red men.

One of these errand-spirits became intimate with one of the young braves, who dwelt in a cabin with his grandmother, and favored him with invitations to stroll with it among the various villages around.

The favor shown by this god to the young man produced a jealousy among his brethren, and during the absence of his distinguished friend, the favored one was much troubled by his neighbors, who envied him his situation.

On one occasion, when this persecution became intolerable, he determined to leave his country, and, if possible, accompany the spirit to the skies.

The chief men had enjoined on all the duty to refrain from any desire or any attempt to ascend the vine whose branches reached the heavens, telling them that to do so would bring upon them severe penalties.

The spirit finding the young man quite sad, inquired, learned the true cause of his sorrow, and taking him, reascended.

The old woman cried for his return, "Noo-sis, be-ge-wain, be-ge-wain." "My child, come back, come back!" He would not come home, and the woman having adjusted all her matters in the lodge, after the nightfall repaired to the vine and began to ascend it.

In the morning the Indians found the lodge she had inhabited empty, and soon espied her climbing the vine. They shouted to her, "Shay! ah-wos be-ge-wain, mah-je-me-di—moo-ga-yiesh!" "Hallo, come back, you old witch you."

But she continued ascending, up—up—up.

A council was held to determine what inducement could be made to her to return. They could hear her sobbing for her grandson. "Ne-gah-wah-bah-mah nos-sis." "I will yet see my child."

Consternation and fear filled the hearts of the Nation, for one of their number was disobeying the Great Spirit. Indignation and fury were seen in the acts of the warriors, and the light of the transgressor's burning wigwam shed its lurid rays around.

The woman was just rearing the top of the vine which was entwined around one of the stars of heaven, and about entering that place, when the vine broke, and down she came, with the broken vine, which had before been the ladder of communication between heaven and earth.

The Nations, as they passed by her, as she sat in the midst of the ruin she had wrought, pushed her declining head, saying, " Whah, ke nah mah dah bee mage men di moo ya yiesh." " There you sit, you wicked old witch."

Some kicked her, others dragged her by her hair,* and thus expressed their disapprobation. All who shall live after thee, shall call thee *Equa* (woman).

The news of this disaster spread rapidly from village to village. Some numbers of men, women, and children

---

* A lady of my acquaintance, quaintly remarked, when I related this story to her. " Yes, the gentleman have been doing that ever since."

were singularly affected. Some complained of pains in their heads, and others of pains in various parts of their bodies. Some were unable to walk, and others equally unable to speak.

They thought some of these fell asleep, for they knew not what death was. They had never seen its presence.

A deep solemnity began its reign in all the villages. There was no more hunting, no more games, and no song was sung to soothe the sun to its evening rest.

Ah, it was then a penalty followed transgression.

Disease was the consequence of the breaking of the vine. Death followed.

One day in the midst of their distress, they consulted each other to determine what could be done. None knew.

They watched carefully for the descent of those beings who used to visit them—and at length they came. Each strove with eagerness to tell his story. They soon found that the strangers were silent and sad.— They asked the Nations what they wished to tell the Great Spirit in their distress.

The first sent a petition that the vine might be replaced between heaven and earth.

The second sent that the Great Spirit might cause the disease to leave them.

The third sent a petition to have the old woman killed, since she was the cause of so much distress.

The fourth desired that the Great Spirit would give them a great deal of game.

The fifth, and last, that the Great Spirit would send them that which would calm and relieve them in distress.

After they had heard these, the strangers left, telling the Indians to wait, and they should know what the Great Spirit should say to each of the petitioners.

Each day of their absence seemed a month. At length they came, and gathered near the eager people They told them that they must die, as the vine that had connected earth to heaven was broken; but the Great Spirit has sent us to release you, and to tell you what you must do hereafter.

The strangers then gathered up all the flowers from the plains, river and lake sides; and after drying them on their hands, blew the leaves with their breath, and they were scattered all over the earth,—wherever they fell, they sprang up and became herbs to cure all disease.

The Indians instituted a dance, and with it a mode of worship. These few, there met, were the first who composed a Medicine Lodge : they received their charter from the Great Spirit, and thus originated the "Medicine Worship."

The strangers gave them these words, and then left

"There is not a flower that buds, however small, that is not for some wise purpose.

There is not a blade of grass, however insignificant, that the Indian does not require.

Learning this, and acting in accordance with these truths, will work out your own good, and will please the Great Spirit."

The above is universally believed by the North West Indians as the origin of Disease and Death, and the foundation of the Medicine Worship.

CHAPTER XIII.

THE Ojibway Nation now occupies land within the bounds of two Governments,—the American and the British. The entire, according to Drake, in 1842, was thirty thousand, which is not far from the truth. The best work upon the Indians of North America, is that deservedly popular book written by Col. McKinney, of New-York, a gentleman of extensive information, and an undoubted friend of the red man.

That part of the Nation occupying territory within the United States, inhabit all the Northern part of Michigan, or the South shore of Lake Huron; the whole Northern portion of Wisconsin Territory; all the South shore of Lake Superior, for eight hundred miles; the upper part of the Mississippi, and Sandy, Leach, and Red Lakes.

Those of the Nation living within the British posses
sions, occupy from Gononaque, below Kingston; all
Western Canada; the North of Lake Huron; the North
of Lake Superior; the North of Lake Winepeg; and
the North of Red River Lake, about one hundred miles.
The whole extent comprises over one thousand nine
hundred miles East and West; and from two to three
hundred miles North and South.

There are about five thousand in the British dominions. In the United States there are about twenty-five
thousand; of whom about five thousand receive religious instruction, from missionaries sent by Societies in
the States and the Canadas.

The first Mission among them was commenced by
the Methodists at Credit River, in Canada West, in
1824, which was followed by a second Mission at Grape
Island in 1827.

The conversion of some Ojibways speedily followed
the introduction of Christianity. Many of these were
sent as native teachers to their brethren in the West.

In 1847, there were twenty-three Methodist Missionary Stations, six of which were in the States, the remainder in Canada. There were four Presbyterian
Missions, all of which were within the States; viz.:
La Pointe, Bad River, Leach Lake, and Red Lake.—

There were seven Episcopalian Mission Stations, six of which were in Canada and one in the United States. Two Baptist Mission Stations ; one at Sault St. Marie, the other at Green Bay. The Roman Catholics had Missionaries in nearly all of the principal places.

Numbers are not under religious instruction, though easily accessible, and are wandering about without the restraints and privileges of the gospel. All around the shores of Lake Superior are bands of Indians who have, time after time, called for Missionaries. The Hudson Bay Company adopted a plan which, in my opinion, did them much credit, by the operation of which instructions were given to the Indians and their children, in the principles of Christianity.

Many persons once belonging to other Nations now live with the Ojibways, and conform to their habits and customs.

The present state of the Ojibways renders them fully ripe and ready for great advancement in religion, literature, and the arts and sciences of civilized life. Multitudes have left their wigwams, their woods, and the attractive chase, and are now endeavoring to tread in the footsteps of worthy white men.

One reason for this change is this—the Chiefs see the necessity of making a " smooth, straight path for their children," and are appropriating as much of their means as they can spare towards doing so.

Another is that the rising generation have imbibed a thirst for learning, and are cultivating a decided taste for improvement in all its branches.

Native teachers being among the people, preaching in their own language, 'Christ and Him crucified,' is a means exceeding all others in their elevation.

The prospects of the Nation have been made brighter through the instrumentality of Missionary effort. Many of the Indians residing in Wisconsin, Lake du Flambeau, the South shore of Lake Superior, and about Winepeg and Red Lakes, have repeatedly requested Missionaries to be sent among them. And these need good teachers, for about the Western part of Red Lake are indeed " the habitations of cruelty." The Chippewas and Siouxs are always at war with each other; the hatred engendered five hundred years ago seems to have lost none of its bitterness.

I will in this place give an account of the Mission Stations in 1842, for which I am mostly indebted to an able report made by Commissioners appointed by Provincial Parliament about that time.

CHIPPEWAS OF THE RIVER THAMES.

JOHN RILEY, CHIEF.

These, together with the Munsees, occupied a tract of land containing about nine thousand acres, in the township of Caradoc, within the London District, at a distance of about twenty-five miles from the Moravian Village. It had been only about ten years since their being reclaimed from a wandering life, and settled at this place. Since 1800, the Munsees had been settled on land belonging to the Chippewas, having received the consent of the Chippewas to locate there. The Chippewas numbered three hundred and seventy-eight ; the Munsees two hundred and forty-two. They were not collected in a village, but lived on small farms, scattered over their tract. Some of the Chippewas cultivated lots of twenty acres each. This tribe occupied seventy-six log houses, six wigwams and twenty-five barns; and had four hundred and fifty acres of land under good cultivation. Their stock consisted of about six hundred head. They had a fanning mill, a blacksmith's shop, and a moderate supply of agricultural tools.

THE CHIPPEWAS AT AMHERSTBURG.

These all professed Christianity, and many of them were examples of true piety. The majority were Wesleyan Methodists ; the minority Romanists. They had no place of worship of their own, though they had the means to erect one had they desired to do so. The Indian settlement is about three miles from the town of Amherstburg. The Methodist minister stationed at Amherstburg, visited those of his persuasion among the Indians, every Sabbath day, and by the aid of an Interpreter preached, read and expounded the scriptures to them. They held a general prayer meeting once a fortnight, and frequent and private meetings for social worship. Many of them maintained family worship. The Roman Catholics worshipped in a chapel at Amherstburg.

There were no schools among them ; but they had expressed a desire to have one established. Persons capable of judging, thought the children no way inferior to those of the whites in their ability to acquire knowledge.

CHIPPEWAS OF THE ST. CLAIR.

WA-WA-NOSH, AND SALT, CHIEFS.

These Indians were among the first whom Sir John Colborne endeavored to settle and civilize. Previous to 1830, they were wandering heathen, like their brethren elsewhere, scattered over the Western part of the Upper Province ; they were drunken and dissipated in their habits and without religious or moral restraint. In 1830-31, a number of them were collected on a Reserve in the township of Sarnia, near the head of the River St. Clair, containing over ten thousand acres. A number of houses were built for them, and an officer was appointed to superintend the settlement.

Their conversion to Christianity and their progress in religious knowledge, and in the acquisition of sober, orderly and industrious habits, had been, under the care of the Wesleyan Methodist Society, both rapid and uniform. From the formation of the Mission to that time, (1842) two hundred and twenty-one adults, and two hundred and thirty-nine children had been baptized and admitted into the community.

In 1840, the total number at this Mission did not exceed three hundred and fifty; but an increase soon followed, owing to the emigration from Saginaw Bay, Michigan, and the settlement of wandering Indians— and at the time of the Commissioners' report, the number was seven hundred and forty-one.

The Indians of River Aux Sables had about sixty acres under improvement, and one log house. Those at Kettle Point, twenty acres and two log houses. The land on the Upper Reserve had been regularly surveyed and laid out in farm lots.

The Chief, with the approval of the Superintendent, placed most of the occupants on these lands ; but it was not indispensable that he should be consulted, as the members of the tribe had the liberty to choose any unoccupied spot, and improve it as their own. When once in possession, they were secured against intrusion, but drunkenness or other ill conduct made them subject to the Chief, who had power to expel them from the Reserve.

CHIPPEWAS AT WALPOLE ISLAND.

These Indians are also known by the name of " the Chippewas of Chenaille Ecarte." Those who have for an indefinite length of time hunted over the waste lands about Chenaille Ecarte and Bear Creek, are a branch of the Nation settled in Sarnia, and are sharers of the same annuity.

The Pottawatamies emigrated from the States. The settlement at Walpole Island was commenced at the close of the American war, when Col. McKie, called by the Indians " White Elk," collected and placed upon the Island which lies at the junction of the River and the Lake St. Clair, the scattered Indians of certain tribes of Chippewas who had fought on the British side. Being left for a number of years without any interference or assistance on the part of the government, they became a prey to the profligate whites settled on the frontier, who, by various frauds, and in moments of intoxication, obtained leases and valuable portions of the Island.

CHIPPEWAS OF THE RIVER CREDIT

J. SAWYER & P. JONES, CHIEFS.

These were a remnant of a tribe which formerly possessed a considerable portion of the Home and the Gore Districts, of which in 1818, they surrendered the greater part, for an annuity of £532.10, reserving only certain small tracts at the River Credit, and at Sixteen and Twelve Mill Creeks. They composed the first tribe converted to Christianity in Upper Canada.

Previous to 1823, they were wandering pagans. In that year, Messrs. Peter and John Jones, the sons of a white Surveyor, and a Mississaga woman, having been converted to Christianity, and admitted members of the Wesleyan Methodist Church, became anxious to redeem their countrymen from their degraded state of heathenism and destitution. They accordingly collected a considerable number together, and by rote and frequent repetitions, taught the first principles of Christianity to the adults, who were too far advanced in years to learn to read and write. In this manner they committed to memory the Lord's Prayer, the Creed, and the Commandments. As soon as the tribes were converted, they perceived the evils attendant on their former state of ignorance and vagrancy. They began to work, which they had not previously done, and recognized the advantage of cultivating the soil; they totally gave up drinking, to which they had been greatly addicted, and became sober, industrious, and consistent Christians.

THE CHIPPEWAS OF ALNWICK.

SUNDAY & SIMPSON, CHIEFS.

These Indians became converts to Christianity in the years 1826—1827. Previous to those years they were pagans, wandering in the neighborhood of Belville, Kingston, and Gananoque, and were known by the name of "the Mississagas of the Bay of Quinte." In the years referred to, two or three hundred were received into the Wesleyan Methodist Church, and settled on Grape Island, in the Bay of Quinte, six miles from Belville. On this island they resided eleven years, subsisting by agriculture and hunting. Their houses were erected partly by their own labor and partly at the expense of the Methodist Mission Society. They numbered twenty-three: besides which they had a commodious

L

building for religious service and school, a room for an infant school, a hospital, and several mechanical establishments.

CHIPPEWAS AT RICE LAKE.

POUDASH, COPWAY & CROW, CHIEFS.

These settlers belong to the same tribe, the Mississagas, or Chippewas of Rice Lake, who, in 1818, surrendered the greater part of the tract now forming the Newcastle District, for an annuity of £740. They have been reclaimed from their primitive wandering life, and settled in their present locations within the last ten or twelve years.

The Rice Lake Settlement is on the Northern side of the Lake, about twelve miles from Peterborough. The number of Indians was one hundred and fourteen.— They possessed about fifteen hundred acres of land, which were divided into lots of fifty acres each; of these eleven hundred and twenty acres were granted in April, 1834, to trustees, who were "to hold the same for the benefit of the Indian tribes in the Province, with a view to their conversion and .civilization." The remaining four hundred and thirty were afterwards purchased by them with their own funds. They had rather more land cleared than had the Indians of Aln-

wick,—about four hundred acres ; but the cultivation
was not so good. The village contained thirty houses,
a number of barns, a school house, and a chapel, to
which was a bell. At this village the head Chief resided. For some time these Indians were under the
charge of an officer appointed by the Indian Department, who assisted in their settlement, but at the time
of the report they had no special Superintendent.

CHIPPEWAS AT MUD LAKE.

NOGEE, IRON & MCRUE, CHIEFS.

The Mud Lake Indians were settled on a point of
land on the Mud or Chemung Lake, sixteen miles
Northwest of Peterborough. They were ninety-four
in number,—possessed twenty dwelling houses, with
three stables—and occupied a grant of sixteen hundred
acres in the township of Smith, made to the New England Company for their benefit, in April, 1837, of which
two hundred acres were well improved.

These Indians were for some time under the manage-
ment of the late Mr. Scott, an agent for the New Eng
land Company, and were members of the Wesleyan
Methodist Church. A chapel was in progress of erection at the village, where there was at the time a Mis
sion-house and a school.

CHIPPEWAS AT BALSAM LAKE.

CRANE, CHIEF.

The Indians of Balsam Lake, numbering ninety, were settled within the Township of Bexley, on a point of land jutting out into Lake Balsam, which is the most Northerly of the chain of Lakes, running Northwest across the back townships of the district of New Castle. The reserve which was granted to them by the English government, comprised twelve hundred and six acres. Of these, two hundred were cultivated. The village was small; composed of about a dozen houses, with out-buildings and a commodious school-house, in which divine service was performed by a resident Methodist Missionary.

In 1843 these Indians became dissatisfied with the climate, and with the quality of the land at Balsam Lake, and purchased six hundred acres on the banks of Lake Scugog, and were making preparations to remove from their old settlement to their new locality. This volunteer movement of theirs evinced how rapid an improvement was going on in their minds; and showed that the spirit of enterprise existed among them, inasmuch as it was made on account of the superiority of the land near Lake Scugog for agricultural purposes.

CHIPPEWAS OF RAMA.

YELLOWHEAD, NA-NAH-GE-SKUNG & BIG SHILLING, CHIEFS.

These Indians formerly occupied the lands about Lake Simcoe, Holland River, and the unsettled country in the rear of the Home District.

General Darling reported of them in 1828, that they had a strong desire to be admitted into the ranks of Christian people, and to adopt the habits of civilized life; and that in these respects they might be classed with the Mississagas of the Bay of Quinte and Rice Lake, but were at that time in a more savage state.

In 1830, Lieutenant Governor Sir J. Colborne collected them on a tract of land on the Northwest shore of Lake Simcoe, where they cleared a road from that lake to Lake Huron. This tract numbered nearly ten thousand acres. They consisted of three tribes of Chippewas, under Chiefs Yellowhead, Aisance, and Snake; and a band of Pottawatomies, from Drummond Island; their number was about five hundred, under the care of Mr. Anderson, who was appointed to take charge of their settlement. They made a rapid advancement.

CHIPPEWAS OF BEAUSOLIEL ISLAND, MATCHADASH BAY, LAKE HURON.

AISANCE & JAMES KA-DAH-GE-GWON, CHIEFS.

This band was the same which was settled by Sir John Colborne, at Cold Water. Their village, which was not far from their former settlement, was commenced in 1841. It contained nearly twenty houses. The settlers numbered two hundred and thirty-two; and had under their own cultivation one hundred acres of land.

The majority of these Indians were Roman Catholics. They had no place for worship or school. The Roman Catholic priest of Penetanguishene made them occasional visits.

CHIPPEWAS OF SNAKE ISLAND, LAKE SIMCOE.

J. SNAKE, CHIEF.

This body of Indians was one of the three bands established at Cold Water and the Narrows, and separated from them on the abandonment of those settlements.

In 1842 they occupied one of the three Islands on Lake Simcoe, which had been set apart for the tribe many years previous. They were over one hundred in number, and occupied twelve dwelling houses. They had other buildings, and a school-house. The children were instructed by a respectable teacher, and Divine service was conducted by a resident Missionary of the Methodist persuation.

They had about one hundred and fifty acres under cultivation, and were rapidly improving in habits of industry and agricultural skill.

Their Missionary, who had been acquainted with them for about three years, stated that the majority of them were strictly moral in their character,—that most of the adults were decidedly pious—and that many of them for consistency of character, would not suffer by a comparison with white Christians of any denomination.

CHIPPEWAS OF SANGEEN (LAKE HURON).

J. METEGOUB, ALEXANDER & AH-YAH-BANCE, CHIEFS.

It was from these Indians, and their brethren, since settled at Owen's Sound, that Sir Francis Head, in 1836, obtained a surrender of a vast tract of land lying North of the London and Gore Districts, and between the Home District and Lake Huron, containing one million six hundred thousand acres. He reserved at the same time, for the Indians, the extensive peninsula, lying between Lake Huron and Georgian Bay, North of Owen's Sound, and supposed to contain four hundred and fifty thousand acres.

CHIPPEWAS OF BIG BAY, IN OWEN'S SOUND, LAKE HURON.

JOHN JONES & WAH-BAH-DEICK, CHIEFS.

These Indians were formerly either wanderers in the Sangeeng tract, surrendered by Sir Francis Head, or lived in scattered wigwams on the shores of Big Bay. An agreement was then made with them, by which it was proposed that they should either repair to Manitonlin, or to that part of their former territory which lies North of Owen's Sound; upon complying with which, it was promised, " that houses should be built for them, and proper assistance given to enable them to become civilized and cultivate the land."

CHIPPEWAS AND OTHERS, IN THE TOWNSHIP OF BEDFORD.

Within a few years previous to 1842, some stragglers from the Rice Lake tribe had settled in the township of Bedford, about twenty-five miles North of the town of Kingston. About that year they were joined by a band of eighty-one Indians from Lower Canada, belonging to the part of the " Lake of Two Mountains."

By instructions issued in 1843, these Indians were transferred from the Roll of Lower Canada to that of the Upper Province. and in the course of that year they received their annual Government presents for the first time in that Province.

CHAPTER XIV.

THE Mission of the Episcopal Church at the Sault St. Marie, was given up soon after the Rev. Mr. Murray left the country, on account of the removal of the Indians from their town to an Island in Lake Huron, by order of Sir Francis Broadhead.

This dignitary gained notoriety among the Indians and the whites of Canada, on account of his attempt to remove the Indians to "a lone barren isle," where those who did go suffered greatly by the bleak winds of the lake.

The soil, what there was of it, was not good enough to raise potatoes, or any vegetables for their support,— its chief productions being large rocks and small stones.

Mr. Murray, it appears, was a man of untiring energy and perseverance. He labored for a number of years as a devoted Missionary, and was finally obliged to leave by the impolitic acts of government.

In the month of September, 1834, I had the pleasure of seeing this gentleman. He was reading an account of his labors to a crowded auditory of Indians, who listened with deep, unfeigned interest, to the relation of the improvements they had made under the care of " the good white man."

One of the most distinguished individuals of the Ojibwas, is *Shin-gwah-koonce.* He is a Chief of much celebrity,—noted for his bravery, activity, and perseverance. His person is a little above the medium size, and well proportioned. His head well formed ; and, to a phrenological eye, pleasing. His general appearance is highly commanding.

He fought with the British during the last war, and was engaged at the storming of Mackanaw, and at the battle of Chippeway. It is said that he retains numerous scars, and such like mementoes of the war of 1822.

The Indians who then lived on the English side of Sault St. Marie, have removed to Manetowahning, on the North shore of Lake Huron, where a Mission has been established by the Episcopal Church. There are also Roman Catholics on the Island. They are by far the most numerous of the Missionaries among the Ojibways.

The Methodists have established their Missions at the Northwest end of Lake Superior.

Fort William is one of the fortresses of the Hudson Bay Company. One of the young men who was educated in Cazenovia, is now the principal minister there. His name is Henry Steinhaux, and he is doing a good work in teaching school and acting in the capacity of Missionary to the Indians of that place.

Norway House is another place in the interior of the country, towards the water of the Red River, where there is a Mission. Peter Jacobs is the most efficient laborer in that country. He has been for a long time very zealously engaged in teaching his less fortunate brethren the first rudiments of education.

A very amusing story is told of Peter Jacobs, the incidents of which occurred at a camp meeting near Belville, about the year 1828.

I must mention that, during the previous summer. several hundred had embraced Christianity. Peter attended the meeting following this conversion. The white people also attended the meeting, and so universal was the diffusion of the Good Spirit, that the pale face and the red man knelt together in prayer to that Great Being

who makes no distinction, but between good and evil.
The ground was covered with people in a devotional
attitude. Peter knelt with them. His companions
were in ecstacies with the presence of Divine favor.—
Peter soon learned the fact that the Great Spirit despis-
ed not even the trembling prayer of the forest child.

Springing upon his feet in an instant, he mounted
one of the benches, and waved his hand to the vast
concourse of people. He then spoke rapidly, eloquently,
and feelingly, as follows :

" The Great Spirit has blest Peter the orphan boy.—
He no tell lies. He says He love me. That good man
say, (pointing to the preacher,) Jesus died for every one.
How happy, happy now ! My father, mother, gone ;
they drank fire-water, (turning to some of the traders,
who were at this moment as attentive as the rest). You
did not give the Indian blessed Bible ; you cheated poor
Indian for his furs. You kill my people. What will
the Great Spirit say when he come ? He will tell you
—' You give poor Indian fire-water : you kept the Bible
from poor Indian, long, long time. *You big rascal go
to Hell.'* That is what he will say to you."

Peter sat down, while the *biggest tradesman* trembled
in his shoes.

The meeting was held near the Bay of Quinte, in

Adolphustown. The above incident in Peter's early experience, was related to me by a gentleman, now living near the place.

Lately Peter went to England, and created considerable interest in behalf of the Northwest Indians, among whom he is now laboring.

The Wesleyan Methodist Missions in the interior, are now altogether supported by the Hudson Bay Company. It has become a well known fact, that, when the Indians are under the influence of Christian Missionaries, the Company have less trouble with individuals in the course of trade. Indians thus instructed, are becoming good farmers and support themselves by labor.

The Hudson Bay Company discountenance the use of fire-water in all the country they occupy. But recently, during the mining operations on the North shore of Lake Superior, liquor has been introduced.

The Indian population of Canada have ever manifested a strong friendly feeling towards the British government.

In former years, the American governors were more kindly disposed to us than they have been of late, yet the name of "Children" is applied to us. The government and its agents style us, "My Children." The Indians are of age—and believe they can think and act for themselves. The term, " My Children," comes with an ill grace from those who seem bent on driving them from their fathers' house.

As yet, the Ojibway Nation in Canada West have not to my knowledge received any encouragement pecuniarily from the government for education. What they have attained has been received by their own efforts. I remember several years ago of being sent to the then Governor of the Province, in Montreal, for aid in our school. All that we received was a nod—which our gracious father deigned to give.

It is more provoking now with us, since we have suffered in name from the acts of the last war, with the British and the Americans. Our fathers fought for the British during these struggles. Now, since these are passed we have been left to ourselves,—and until the government require our services, shall remain uncared for. Your British subjects may say, ' Do we not give you blankets, and clothe you and your children ?' But what amount of land has not our people given to the government since they became so poor ?

And if the benevolent of the United States had not given us education, many of us would have been still wandering in the woods of Canada without the means of religious education. We don't want merely blankets to cover the body,—we want Light! We want Education!

For several years I have been denied receiving any presents from the British government,—consisting of a blanket, a shirt, and leggins—because I had been *too much with the Americans*, the enemies of the British government. I would rather never see a blanket again. Think how small for a man to be bought with a blanket!

The whole of the Indian population of Canada West is improving rapidly. The bands are uniting, and will not in future be so isolated as formerly.

The writer in 1844 and 1845, endeavored to convince his brethren of many advantages they would derive by being in large communities. Through his influence the Chiefs of Owen's Sound, and Sahageeng, made their offer to the scattered bands of Indians throughout the Western country.

At the General Council, to which allusion was made in a previous chapter, it was suggested that a meeting of the small villages be made at the following places— Rice Lake, in New Castle District; in Muncytown, London District; and in Owen's Sound Bay, in the Eastern part of Lake Huron.

This meeting the Indians have already commenced.

Several villages have been abandoned, and their tenants departed to the places above specified.

In the winter seasons sleigh rides are popular, and visits to neighboring tribes, in large bodies, are quite frequent.

Christmas and New Year's dinners are, with the Ojibways, occasions of much merriment.

The village of Alnwich is one side of the Lake, and that of Rice Lake opposite. The distance between them is about seven miles. Chief John Sandy orders his warriors to give a dinner to the other tribe on Christmas—and they in return give a dinner to Sandy's tribe on New Year's day.

In 1848, I was present, at my father's village, Rice Lake, when one of these dinners took place. In point of order, social mirth, and real enjoyment, it was equal to any aldermanic festivity among the whites.

M

CHAPTER XV.

THE early discovery of the Northwest has been a subject of considerable interest—and as there is much valuable information in the following, which we take from one of the Minesota Territory papers, prepared by the Rev. Edward D. Neill, the research which is here found will be apparent. If the missionary field was blessed with more such men, it would augment its interests in the mind of the literary world. It is to be hoped that he will continue to give such information from time to time for the general good.

"The journals of the first missionaries to the Hurons were perused with like enthusiasm by the kings, queens, statesmen, merchants, artizans, and peasants of Papal Europe. The lovers of romance wept freely over the sufferings of the priests, and the reported conversion of so many to the faith. The enterprizing merchant encouraged the missions that were opening so many new avenues of trade.

Before proceeding to a sketch of the explorers and explorations in Minesota during the seventeenth century, let us rapidly glance at the progress of discovery in the countries adjacent. As early as 1634, the Indians had learned to bring their furs to Quebec, and received European manufactures in exchange. In September of that year, two priests, Brebœuf and Daniel, determined to accompany a party of Hurons to their forest home, and teach them the doctrines of the Christian religion. They were the first Europeans that erected a house in the neighborhood of Lake Huron.

Seven years after, a bark canoe, containing priests of the same order, passed through the river Ottawa, and coasted along the shores of Lake Huron, to visit, by invitation, the Ojibways, at the outlet of Lake Superior. After a voyage of seventeen days, they arrived at the Falls of St. Mary, where they found assembled two thousand of that tribe, who now dwell in the North-eastern portion of our Territory.

While here, they obtained much information, calculated to inflame the zeal of the Society of Jesus, and their patrons in Europe. Here, for the first time, civilized man learned that the Nation of Dakotas, amid whose lodges we reside, was in existence. The Ojibways informed the missionaries that the Dakotas lived eighteen days' journey farther to the West.

Thus, says Brancroft, in his eloquent chapter on Jesuit Missions, ' did the religious zeal of the French, bear the cross to the banks of the St. Mary, and the confines of Lake Superior, and look wistfully toward the home of the Sioux in the Valley of the Mississippi, five years before the apostle Eliot had addressed the tribe of Indians that dwelt within six miles of Boston Harbor.'

Either accompanying the missionary, devoted to a life of poverty, or in his immediate rear, followed the trader, devoted to a life of gain ; so that a chapel was hardly surmounted with a cross, before a trading house stood by its side. In the year 1654, two adventurous young men, connected with the fur trade, followed a party of Indians in their hunting excursions for two years, and were probably the first white men that ever penetrated the Dakota country.

Upon their return to Quebec, they gave such glowing accounts of the lands they had seen, the lakes they had crossed, the Nations they had become acquainted with, among whom were the Sioux or Dakotas, that both trader and ecclesiastic burned with desire to go up and possess the land. Even the Bishop of Quebec was ready to be the pioneer in planting the symbol of his faith among the newly discovered tribes. But it was at length decided that the aged Mesnard, who had obtained dearly purchased experience among the Indians of Western New-York, should carry the religion of Rome to the shores of Lake Superior. With an ardor that every one must admire, he loitered not after his appointment, but leaving the pleasant society of his associates, he pushed onward to his field of labor, to use his own language, trusting 'in the Providence which feeds the little birds of the desert, and clothes the wild flowers of the forest,' and expecting that his friends would shortly add him 'to the memento of deaths.'

Hoping against hope, he reached the shores of Superior in safety. After residing on the Southern shore of the Lake about eight months, he started on a journey for the Bay of Che-goi-me-gon. But one person accompanied him, and while his companion was making, as it is supposed, what is called the Keweena Portage, Mesnard was lost in the forest. Whether he died from starvation, exposure, or the tomahawk, has never been discovered. There is a tradition that his cassock and prayer book were kept as amulets for many years by the Dakotas. The melancholy disappearance of this aged soldier of the church, did not deter Claude Allouez, also a Jesuit, from visiting the shores of Lake Superior, in the year 1665.

At that early date, there were rumors that there was a large mass of copper on the Southern shore, but his search for it was unavailing. Pushing beyond Ontanagon, the adventurous man did not stop until he reached the Island of La Pointe, the ancient residence of the Ojibways, who were then as often times now, planning a war party against their enemies, the Dakotas. He then must be regarded as the first white man of whom we have authentic account, who first trod the soil on the confines of Minesota. According to the Ojibway tradition, the first white men at La Pointe were traders, who had been confined by the ice, and were found in a starving condition, eating their cloth and blankets. Yet, that priests were here at a very early period, is very certain from the fact that a small silver crucifix of antique workmanship, has been lately ploughed up in that vicinity. At that period the territory of the Dakotas extended quite to the shores of Superior; and Allouez in his intercourse with them, was the first to learn of the existence of a great river which he calls the 'Messipi.'

During his two years residence in the Northwest, he

founded the Mission of the Holy Spirit, and passed his time in teaching the Ojibways the 'Pater Noster' and 'Ave Maria ;' in endeavoring to awaken their slumbering consciences by pictures of hell and the judgment day, and in obtaining information from the Sioux or Dakota Nation.

His labors were so successful, that he returned to Quebec to solicit assistants, but his heart remained with the Ojibways, and in two days he was on his return route, accompanied by a fellow-laborer, named Nicolas.

In 1668 he was cheered by the arrival of two others, named Dablon and Marquette, the latter of whom was destined to become known by posterity.

Marquette, during his missionary tours in the vicinity of Lake Superior, had heard so much of the 'great river Messipi,' that he determined to take the first favorable opportunity to discover it.

On the 10th of July, 1673, in company with a French Envoy, and five others, they left the Mission at Green Bay, ascended the Fox River, made a portage, and descended the Wisconsin. After paddling the birch canoes for seven days, without meeting man or beast, they reached its mouth and floated on the bosom of the 'Father of Waters.' Fearing nothing, excited by the very danger of the adventure.

' Day after day they glided adown the turbulent river;
Night after night, by their blazing fires, encamped on its borders.
Now through rushing chutes, among green islands where plume-like
Cotton-trees nodded their shadowy crests, they swept with the current,
Then emerged into broad lagoons, where silvery sand-bars
Lay in the stream, and along the rippling waves of their margin,
Shining with snow-white plumes, large flocks of pelicans waded.
They were approaching the region where reigns perpetual summer.'

Nor did they cease descending, until they left the Wisconsin eleven hundred miles above them. Returning by the way of the Illinois river to Chicago, they proceeded by Lake Michigan to Green Bay, where they arrived about the last of September. This voyage excited much conversation and speculation, in old as well as new France.

At this time there dwelt in Canada, a native of Rouen, named La Salle, who not only possessed an adventurous disposition, but was also a man of foresight, determination, and finished education. While a student at a Jesuit College in France, he was distinguished for his proficiency in mathematics.

At the time of Marquette's return from the Mississippi, he was living at his trading post at the junction of the St. Lawrence with Lake Ontario, where the town of Kingston stands. Around Fort Frontenac, for that was the name of the post, there were gathered a few French families and priests.

The more La Salle dwelt upon the discovery of Marquette and Joliet, the greater his eagerness to complete
what had been commenced, and to discover what he
believed to exist, a short route to China and Japan from
the head waters of the Mississippi. To obtain the
patronage of Louis XIV., he sailed for France, and in
the year 1678 received permission to make discoveries
in the Western part of New France, to build forts
wherever they were necessary, and the exclusive right
to the trade in Buffalo skins, which were just beginning
to be known and valued in Europe.

Among the priests at Frontenac, was a native of
Flanders, a Franciscan of the meditative order, styled
Recollect. From early life, he evinced a roving disposition, and the stories of the sailors who used to enter
the harbors of Calais and Dunkirk, where he had resided, are said to have created a strong desire in him
to see the new world.

His name was Louis Hennepin ; vain, boasting, and
ambitious, he suffers by comparison with the meek, un-
ostentatious, and comparatively truthful Marquette.—
While La Salle was absent, the Franciscan passed his
time in missionary tours among the Iroquois, and is
said to have visited the present capital of the State of
New-York. When La Salle returned from France, he

despatched a small vessel to Niagara river, laden with
materials for building a ship suitable for navigating the
Lakes. Among the passengers was Hennepin, who
with eight others landed and travelled some thirty
leagues through the woods, to hold a council with the
Senecas, whose good will they obtained.

On the 20th of January, 1679, La Salle joined the
party, encamped on the shores of the Niagara river, and
strained every nerve in making preparations for a great
Western voyage. In a week, a dock yard was not only
selected, but the keel of a ship laid. The builders plied
the adze and the hammers vigorously, though in fear
that the Indians would apply the torch to their work
and the tomahawk to their scalps. When they began
to murmur, Father Hennepin began to exhort, and as
he says, ' allay their fears.'

In six months, the vessel was ready for launching.
It was named the Griffin, in compliment to Count Frontenac, the Governor of Canada, whose armorial bearings
were adorned by two griffins. It was defended by a
few guns, and ornamented by an eagle and a griffin on
its prow.

By means of ropes, the vessel was towed from the
Niagara River to Lake Erie, much to the astonishment
of the natives. On the 7th of August, 1679, La Salle,

Hennepin, and some thirty others, entered the ship and spread their sails to the breeze. The waters of Lake Erie bore the vessel most gallantly, and in three days they were within the vicinity of the spot, where now stands the city of Detroit. Passing through the Lake, which they named St. Clair, in honor of one of the saints of the Church of Rome, they entered Lake Huron. Here they encountered one of those terrible storms, which even the experienced sailor of modern days dreads. All but the pilot, who according to Hennepin, was destitute of religious feeling, began to pray to the Patron Saint, Anthony of Padua. But not a hair of their heads was injured; the waves at last fell to sleep, and upon the 27th of the month they safely moored in one of the harbors of Mackinaw Island.

Here Hennepin, and the other ecclesiastics, celebrated mass, and La Salle, wrapped in a scarlet cloak edged with gold, visited the assembled Indians. This being a desirable point for trade with the tribes, a fort was built. Leaving Mackinaw, they entered Lake Michigan, and anchored at an island at the mouth of Green Bay. In two weeks time the Griffin was freighted with furs to the amount of twelve thousand dollars, and sent back to Niagara, which point she never reached, and as it was supposed, was wrecked in another storm.

Leaving Green Bay in four birch canoes, La Salle and his followers coasted along the Eastern boundary of Wisconsin, and at last pitched their tents in the neighborhood of Milwaukie river. Fatigued and without a supply of food, they were much disheartened ; but the Indians in the vicinity proved friendly, and administered to their wants.

After being exposed to many perils by land and by water, they landed on the first of November at the mouth of the river St. Joseph in Michigan. Late in the season they started from thence for the Illinois river; but before they reached that stream, provisions again grew scarce. In their extremity, Providence assisted ; for, says Hennepin, a stray Buffalo was found sticking fast in a marsh, which served for food. After a journey of three hundred miles, they at last reached the Illinois, and descended to an Indian village situated near the present town of Ottawa. Winter being at hand, the inhabitants were on their annual hunt ; but the travellers, pressed with hunger, could not refrain from helping themselves to some of the corn.

They continued to proceed down the river, until the first of January, 1680, when they halted, and had a new year's celebration, consisting of religious services by Hennepin and other priests.

The ceremonies being over, they entered Lake Peoria, at the lower end of which they discovered an encampment of Indians. After the red men had recovered from their astonishment, they invited the strangers to their cabins, and passed the day in feasting.

La Salle told them that he had come to impart a knowledge of the true God, and to supply them with fire arms, in the place of the awkward weapons they had been accustomed to use. The night after he made this speech, a Chief of a tribe residing on Fox River, stole into the camp, and calling the Chiefs together, told them that he had been informed that the Frenchmen were allied with their old enemies, the Iroquois. This false intelligence communicated to the Indians by La Salle's enemies, produced much consternation. The next morning, in the place of cordiality, the travellers found only coldness and suspicion. The commander inquired the cause of the sudden change, and he was then told the whole tale. A man of uncommon tact and address, he soon regained their confidence. He now began to inquire about the Mississippi, and spoke of his plan of building a boat, after the white man's fashion, to sail upon that stream. The principal men of the camp did not fully approve of his plan, and they attempted to dissuade him, by saying, ' that the banks of the Mississippi were inhabited by a gigantic race of men, who killed all travellers ; that it was filled with crocodiles, serpents and monsters, as well as falls and rapids, and that there was a dreadful whirlpool at its mouth.'

The discernment of La Salle convinced him that this was what we vulgarly term a ' hoax,' and he arose and told the spokesman, that his sayings were stamped with improbability. These stories, however, caused six of the company to desert and others to complain.

As it was now too cold to travel with comfort, the erection of a fort was commenced not far distant from the town of Peoria

Here, in the interior of the North American Continent, two years before the Quaker Penn purchased of the Indians the spot where the city of Philadelphia now stands, might be heard the sound of the saw, the blowing of the forge, the stroke of the sledge, and the ring of the anvil. In less than six weeks, and in the midst of winter, this exploring band had erected a log fort, which they named Crevecœur, and the hull of a vessel 42 feet long and 12 broad, which was to have been employed in navigating the Mississippi. The necessary cordage and rigging being absent, the ship could not be completed.

But La Salle was still intent upon discovering a short route to the ' wealth of Ormus and of Ind,' and therefore ordered Father Hennepin to proceed on a voyage to the sources of the Mississippi.

This was not unwelcome intelligence to the forward Franciscan ; and on the last day of February, 1680, with one canoe laden with goods, and two companies, Picard du Gay and Michel Ako, he began his long and dangerous journey.

In seven days he had reached the mouth of the Illinois ; but on account of the floating ice, he had to wait some time before he could ascend the ' Meschasipi,' as he termed the river upon the banks of which we dwell. By the 11th of April, he had paddled as far as the Wisconsin river, in the vicinity of which he met a flotilla of canoes, filled with Issati or Dakota Indians, called Issati or Issanti, as it is supposed, after their ancient residence at Mille Lac. With them he passed through the Lac des Pleurs, shortly after called Pepin, which name it still retains, which he thus describes. ' About thirty leagues above Black River, we found the Lake of Tears, which we named so, because the savages who took us, as it will be hereafter related, consulted in this place what they should do with their prisoners, and those who were for murdering cried all night upon us, to oblige by their tears, their companions to consent to our death. This lake is formed by the "Meschasipi," and may be seven leagues long and five broad.'

As the Dakotas were generally very kind in the treatment of their white captives, very little credence can be given to the tale of the Father's captivity.

After nineteen days' travel with the Indians, he discovered a cataract, which he says 'indeed of itself is terrible, and hath something very astonishing.' He reported the falls to be sixty feet in height, which is quite moderate for the man who published those at Niagara to be six hundred feet. Near the cataract was a bearskin upon a pole, a sort of oblation to the spirit in the waters.

After carving the cross and the arms of France on a tree, and calling them after the Patron Saint of the expedition, the eloquent divine, Anthony of Padua, he abandoned his canoe and journeyed by land to the residence of the Indians, on a stream, which, in honor of the founder of his order, he called St. Francis.* Their manner of welcoming a stranger at that time, seems to have been very peculiar. Says Hennepin, ' at the entry of the Chief's cabin, who had adopted me, one of the barbarians, who seemed to be very old, presented me

* Now called Elk River.

with a pipe to smoke, and weeping over me all the
while with abundance of tears, rubbed both my hands
and my head. This was to show how concerned he
was to see me so harrassed and fatigued. And indeed
I had often need enough of two men to support me,
when I was up, or raise me when I was down. There
was a bear's skin before the fire, upon which the youngest boy of the cabin caused me to lie down, and then
with the grease of wild-cats, anointed my thighs, legs,
and soles of my feet.'

The first of white men then, who looked upon the
Falls of St. Anthony, was not a Jesuit, as Steinmetz,
misled by Kip's eloquent preface to the 'early Jesuit
Missions in North America,' asserts ; but a Franciscan
of the Recollect branch.

While Hennepin was dwelling upon the banks of the
St. Francis, he was agreeably surprised by the arrival
of a party of French traders from Lake Superior, under
the direction of a Sieur de Luth, and probably among
the first who had ever penetrated so far into the interior
of the Dakota country. About the last of September,
1680, the whites left the Indian village, and descending
the Mississippi as far as the Wisconsin, they proceeded
by way of that stream, and Green Bay, to Quebec.—
Hennepin did not tarry long in that city, but went to
N

France, and in 1683, published a book of travels under the title of 'A Description of Louisiana,' as all of the Valley of the Mississippi was then called.

Had the restless Franciscan remained contented with the reputation acquired by the discovery of the Falls of St. Anthony, posterity would have viewed his exaggerations and misstatements with a kindly eye, and remembered his name with pleasure.

But in an evil hour, he was tempted to claim the honor of not only discovering the source, but the mouth of the Mississippi ; and to sustain the claim, he contradicted what he had previously asserted, and committed one of the meanest plagiarisms on record. After the renowned La Salle had met an untimely end, by the hand of a conspirator, La Clercq published the letters of Fathers Zenobe and Anastase, giving a description of the scenery and productions of the lower Mississippi. Hennepin, with the aid of these missionary letters, and a fertile imagination, prepared a book entitled 'New Discovery of a vast Country situated in America, between New Mexico and the Frozen Ocean.' In this he is daring enough to state, that he paddled a canoe with the aid of two men, from the Illinois to the Gulf o_ Mexico, and back, more than two thousand five hundred miles, in forty-nine days.

Anticipating the query from some inquisitive French-
man, ' why did you not say something about the discovery of the mouth of the Mississippi, in your first
work, published more than ten years since ?' he frames
a most awkward and insufficient apology. After stating
that La Salle was envious and jealous of him, he remarks that he was also unfriendly, because during his
first voyage to France, when a gay company of young
women commenced dancing upon the deck of the ship,
he had reprimanded them for their gaiety ; La Salle,
who was a fellow passenger, interposed and said there
was no harm in dancing, and that the Franciscan had
overstepped the bounds of his authority. Warm words
ensued, and we are called upon to believe that by this
frivolous incident, a root of bitterness was planted in
his bosom which was never eradicated.

None of his excuses sustained Hennepin's reputation ;
and shortly after we find him, in his old age, leaving
France. Crossing the Channel, he published in London another edition of his real and fictitious discoveries
in the Valley of the Mississippi, and staunch Romanist
as he professed to be, entered into the pay of England's
Protestant King, William III., who was anxious to be
the rival of France in colonizing the banks of the Mississippi, and willing ' to leap over twenty stumbling
blocks rather than not effect it.'

As a town in the State of Illinois, has already taken the name of Hennepin, which would have been so appropriate for our neighboring and beautiful village of St. Anthony, we take leave of the discoverer of those picturesque Falls, which will always render that town equally attractive to the eye of the poet and capitalist, by suggesting, that the island which divides the 'laughing waters,'* be called Hennepin, who though, as Bancroft says, ' a boastful liar,' was nevertheless a ' daring discover.'

Eight years after Hennepin announced the discovery of the Falls of St. Anthony to his friends in Canada, another exploration of the Valley of the Upper Mississippi was undertaken by Baron Lahontan. About the last of September, 1688, with a large party of French and Indians, he departed with his heavily laden canoes from the fort at Mackinaw, and proceeded by the usual and natural route by Green Bay, Fox and Wisconsin Rivers, to the Mississippi, upon whose waters he floated on the 23d of October. Ascending this stream, he says that on the 3d of November, he entered into a river that was almost without a current, and at its mouth filled with rushes. He remarks moreover, that he ascended

---

* The Dakota Indians call the Falls of St. Anthony, " Rara," from Lrara, to laugh.

it for more than five hundred miles. Upon its banks
dwelt three Nations : the Eokoros, Essannapes, and the
Guacsitares. On account of its great length, having
been employed sixty days in its ascent, he named it
Riviere Longue. As there is no stream in existence
that answers to the description, many have been inclined
to look upon the account of Baron Lahontan, in the
same light as they view the stories of Baron Munchau-
sen. Others, more credulous, have credited him with
the discovery of the Minesota or Saint Pierre River.—
Nicollet supposes that the Riviere Longue of Lahontan
was Cannon River, which enters the Mississippi near
the head of Lake Pepin, and that this stream was then
an outlet of the Minesota. A reference to the map,
shows that there is but a short distance between the
sources of Cannon River, and the Le Sueur and other
tributaries of the Mankato or Blue Earth Rivers.

Bradford in his ' Notes on the North West,' agrees
with Nicollet. He remarks—' there is very clear evidence, from geological indications, that the whole Upper
Mississippi was at one time submerged ; and it is highly
probable, that in the gradual subsidence of the waters
which may not have taken place in 1690 or 1700, to
the extent it has now attained, a great lake may have
covered all that area.

The supposition that he passed through Cannon River is not improbable. The sources of Cannon River are within four or five miles of an Eastern branch of Blue Earth River, and the intervening ground is a perfect level. The communication may at the time of the voyage have been complete, or been made so by a freshet, and he would thus have passed through the Blue Earth into St. Peter's River.*

Keating supposed that the Hoka or Root River, was the one referred to by Lahontan, and remarks, 'it is impossible to read the Baron Lahontan's account of this river, without being convinced that the greater part, if not the whole of it, is a deception.' When doctors disagree, it would be vain for us to attempt to decide.

* 'Having procured a copy of Lahontan's book, in which there is a roughly made map of his Long River, I was struck with the resemblance of its course as laid down, with that of Cannon River, which I had previously sketched in my own field book. I soon convinced myself that the principal statements of the Baron in reference to the country, and the few details he gives of the physical character of the river, coincide remarkably with what I had laid down, as belonging to Cannon River.'

Thus the lakes and swamps corresponded: traces of Indian villages mentioned by him might be found in the growth of a wild grass that propagates itself around all old Indian settlements. His account of the mouth of the river is particularly accurate. 'We entered the mouth of this Long River, which is a sort of large lake filled with cane brakes, in the midst of which we discovered a narrow channel, which we followed up.'—(NICOLETT's REPORT.

Lahontan having navigated the streams in this region, (perhaps the St. Peter's River,) descended the Mississippi as far as the junction of the Ohio.

Upon his return, he stopped at Fort Crevecœur, on the Illinois, the post from which Hennepin had departed in 1680, on his exploring tour to the sources of the Mississippi.

Though La Salle had been cruelly murdered by a member of his exploring party, his f.iend, Count Frontenac, the Governor of Canada, continued to prosecute with vigor, discoveries, and the establishment of commercial relations with the Indian tribes in the Mississippi valley.

In 1695, he deputed a Monsieur Le Sueur, to build a fort on an island in the Mississippi, in order that peaceful relations might be maintained with the Ojibways and Dakotas. Returning to Montreal, a Chief from each of these then, as now warlike tribes, accompanied him. While in that city, the Dakota Chief, the first that had ever been there, with much ceremony, presented to the Governor as many arrows as his Nation had villages, and entreated that his tribe might enjoy the same privileges of trade as other Indian Nations.

Le Sueur brought back the news, that there were mines of lead and copper in the Sioux country, and hastened to France to lay the information before Louis XIV.

Entirely successful in his application for a grant to work the mines, he left Europe in 1697 ; but just as he came in sight of Newfoundland, the ship in which he was sailing, was captured by the British, and the passengers carried as captives to Portsmouth. The next year he was released, and returned to Paris. Receiving a fresh patent, he started anew to explore the mines, believed to be not many miles distant from the spot on which we dwell. After he arrived in Canada, it was impossible for him to execute his plans, and he returned a third time to the mother country.

The commencement of the year 1699, found a distinguished Canadian in the naval service of the French Government. His name was Iberville, and with several ships and a company of colonists, he went forth to establish a settlement on the Mississippi. They built a fort eighty miles Northeast of New Orleans, and here in 1700 we find Le Sueur, who appears to have possessed indomitable perseverance.

By the order of Iberville, Le Sueur, with a company of ninety men, proceeded to explore the mines in the Dakota country, of which he had given an account five years before. On the first of September, 1700, he had reached the mouth of the Wisconsin. Fourteen days after this, he was at the entrance of the Chippewa, on a

branch of which he had said he had discovered a lump
of copper weighing sixty pounds. Passing through Lac
des Pleurs, which at that early date had begun to be
called Lake Pepin, he reached, on the 16th of September, the mouth of a river, where a Monsieur St. Croix
was drowned, and in memory of whom, it received the
name it now bears. Three days after this, he entered
the Minesota or St. Peter's River, which was not mentioned by Hennepin, the sight of it as he ascended the
stream, being obscured perhaps by the island which is
at its mouth.

Carver informs us that when he visited this country
in 1766, there were on the Eastern side of Lake Pepin,
the ruins of a trading post, that had been in early days
under the superintendence of a captain St. Pierre, and
after him, probably, did Le Sueur call the Minesota
River.*

On the first of October, Le Sueur had ascended the
Minesota to the mouth of the Mankato or Blue Earth
River, about one hundred and fifty miles above Fort
Snelling. He there erected a trading post or fort, which
did not give satisfaction to the Kapoja and other bands

* Since the above was written, we find the following statement in
Nicolett's Report :—' As for my part, I have no hesitation in assigning its origin to a Canadian, by the name of St. Pierre.'

of Dakotas in our vicinity. They claimed that the fort should have been on their lands, at the confluence of the Minesota and Mississippi, where Mendota, the post of the Fur Company, is now situated ; because they were the first with whom the French had traded and furnished with fire arms. The fort was called L'Huillier, after a scientific Parisian, and is said to be marked upon a map published at Amsterdam in 1720.

Having completed the necessary buildings, on the 26th of October, with three canoes, he proceeded to the locality where the Blue Earth was found. After passing the winter in digging, he returned with several thousand pounds of this bluish green earth, to the mouth of the Mississippi, from whence four thousand pounds were transported to France, where it appears to have been of the same value as the sand of the Virginia colonists in England, a century previous.

In the vicinity of the Blue Earth, were said to be mines of copper ; but geologists and others, who have lately explored the country, while they describe the blue pigment used by the Indians, say not a word about any metalic deposits on the Blue Earth River or its tributaries.

With Le Sueur, the French explorations in Minesota appear to have ceased. It is stated that the white residents were obliged to leave the country in 1720, on account of the hostility of the Dakotas. Though this may have contributed to their departure, yet no doubt many traders were impoverished by the bursting of the celebrated Mississippi Company, projected by the infamous swindler, John Law. The professed object of this association was the aggrandizement and cultivation of the colonies of France in North America ; and the French Government enhanced its delusive credit, by assigning to it the whole Territory of Louisiana, of which this country was a district."

CHAPTER XVI.

"The first British traveller to the Falls of St. Anthony, in the introduction to his book of travels, expresses the opinion, 'that at some future period,' the then uncultivated wilderness would become the abode of a civilized people, and 'that stately palaces, and solemn temples with gilded spires reaching to the skies,' would 'supplant the Indian huts, whose only decorations are the barbarous trophies of their vanquished enemies,' and hopes that he may be gratefully remembered by the future inhabitants, as one of those who first visited and described the country now called Minesota. In the place of the skin-lodge of the Dakota, and the oblations to the Spirit supposed to dwell in the roaring waters, we witness this evening, (assembled in a hall dedicated to the purposes of education and unsectarian religion,) an audience, descendants of the old, blue-eyed, energetic Saxon,

clad in robes which their Atlantic forefathers would
have esteemed princely, and dwellers in comfortable
houses, situated upon beautiful eminences which the
Architect of the Universe has been 'smoothing down'
for centuries, and preparing for the abode of a Christian
people.

As it is the chief design of your association to impart
useful information, it is proposed as an introductory
lecture, to give a review of the principal French, British
and American travels to the Falls of St. Anthony.

After noticing the tour of Father Hennepin, Mr. N.
remarked that the next visiter to the Falls, of whom we
have any account, is Jonathan Carver, a captain of a
company of Provincial troops during the war between
Great Britain and France. After the conquest of Canada, and the peace of 1783, he passed some time in an
exploring tour through the Northwest; filled with the
same idea that pervaded the minds of Hennepin and
La Salle, the discovery of a short passage to the Pacific
Ocean. He was convinced, and the late settlement of
the Pacific coast has shown that he was correct, that
the establishment of a colony on the Western coast of
America, 'would not only disclose new sources of trade
and promote many useful discoveries, but would open a
passage for conveying intelligence to China and the

English settlements in the East Indies with greater expedition than a tedious voyage by the Cape of Good Hope or straits of Magellan will allow of.'

Leaving the city of Boston in June 1766, he proceeded by way of Albany and the Lakes to Mackinaw, which was the Northernmost British post. On the 3d of September, he departed from this fort, and on the 18th arrived at Green Bay, the site of the old French Mission and Fort, where in the latter part of the previous century, men educated in the schools of France and accustomed to the polished society of the Courts of Europe, used to assemble and talk over their discoveries and travels. While in this vicinity, he visited an island inhabited by Ottawas, and though deploring the effect of spirituous liquors upon the savage, made a present of some to the Chief, with which the tribe made themselves drunk.

Leaving Green Bay, he proceeded up the Fox River till he came to a town of the Winnebagoes, situated on an island at the eastern end of Lake Winnebago. He asserts that a female presided over this tribe, and describes her as 'a very ancient woman, small in stature and not much distinguished by her dress from several young women that attended her. Her attendants seemed greatly pleased whenever I showed any tokens of respect to their Queen, particularly when I saluted her, which I frequently did to acquire her favor. On these occasions, the good old lady endeavored to assume a juvenile gaiety, and by her smiles showed she was equally pleased with the attention I paid her.'

Carver, like most travellers of olden times, has many curious conceits, and supposes that the Winnebagoes were originally from Mexico, being driven North by the conquests of the Spaniards. He bases his opinion upon the following data : ' their unalienable attachment to the Sioux, the peculiarity of their dialect, and their inveterate hatred of the Spaniards.' After making a portage, he descended the Wisconsin. On the 9th October, he entered a town of the Sauk Indians, where he saw great quantities of lead brought from the mines which are now so extensively worked in Wisconsin. On the 15th of October, he reached the Mississippi. Near the mouth of the Wisconsin he found the town of ' Prairie des Chiens, or Dog Plains.'

This village he thus describes : ' it contains about three hundred families. The houses are well built after the Indian manner. It is the great mart where all the adjacent tribes and even those who inhabit the most remote branches of the Mississippi, trade.'

Having bought a canoe, he proceeded on the 19th of

October, in company with a French Canadian and a Mohawk up the Mississippi. After some difficulty with a band of Pillagers, he arrived, on the first of November, at Lake Pepin. On the East bank of this Lake, he observed the ruins of a French factory, where it is said Captain St. Pierre resided, and carried on a very great trade with the Naudowessies, (Sioux or Dakotas.)— While taking a walk a few miles below Lake Pepin, he found some elevations that had apparently been thrown up for military defence. He says, ' notwithstanding it was now covered with grass, I could plainly discern that it had once been a breast-work of about four feet in height, extending the best part of a mile. I have given as exact an account as possible of this singular appearance, and leave to future explorers of these distant regions to discover whether it is a production of nature or art.'

Featherstonaugh, a United States geologist, about fifteen years ago, visited the spot, and came to the conclusion that it was a work of art, thrown up by some unknown Nation.

Not far distant from the River St. Croix, Carver met a band of Sioux, and while encamped with them, a party of Chippewa warriors came to wage war. The Sioux being alarmed, begged the Captain's assistance. He then visited the Chippewas, from whom he received a friendly reception, and succeeded in persuading them to retire.

About two miles below St. Paul, he saw a remarkable cave, called by the Indians the dwelling of the Great Spirit. The entrance was about ten feet wide and five feet high. About twenty feet from the entrance was a lake, the water of which was transparent. He found in this cave many Indian hieroglyphics, which appeared very ancient, for time had nearly covered them with moss. For many years the mouth of this cave has been filled up with gravel and sand ; but in July, 1837, after much digging, Nicollet succeeded in making an entrance, and saw Indian marks on the wall.

Not far distant from the cave was an Indian burying place, and this fact will help us to account for some of the mounds on the farm of Mr. Weld. Just below the cave resided the Kaposia, or Little Crow band of Indians, who now live four miles below St. Paul, on the West side of the river.

He also gives an interesting, if not a reliable account, of the burial ceremonies that were performed at this cave in the vicinity of St. Paul, and the purport of the harangues made to the deceased.

Having abandoned his canoe opposite the mouth of

O

the St. Peter's River, on account of the ice, he travelled
by land to the Falls of St. Anthony, at which place he
arrived on the 17th of November, 1766. In company
with him was his Mohawk servant, and a young Winnebago Chief. He says he heard the roaring of the
waters at a distance of fifteen miles. As soon as the
Winnebago reached the point below the village of St.
Anthony, which overlooks the Falls, he began to address the Great Spirit, supposed to reside in yon waters.
He told him that he had come a long way to pay his
adorations and offerings to him ; after which, he threw
his pipe, tobacco-pouch, bracelets, beads, ear-rings, and
all that he esteemed valuable, into the boiling waters.

Carver states the Falls to be two hundred and fifty
yards wide, and the perpendicular fall to be thirty feet.
In the middle of the Falls, was an island as at present,
and half way between the side on which we stand and
the island, there was a rock, lying at the very edge of
the Falls, in an oblique position, that appeared to him
to be about five or six feet broad, and thirty or forty
feet long.

With the surrounding scenery he was as delighted as
the most enthusiastic citizen of St. Anthony could desire. His description is as follows : ' The country
around them is extremely beautiful. It is not an unin-

terrupted plain where the eye finds no relief, but composed of many gentle ascents, which in the summer are covered with the finest verdure, and interspersed with little groves that give a pleasing variety to the prospect. On the whole, when the Falls are included, which may be seen at the distance of four miles, a more pleasing and picturesque view cannot, I believe, be found throughout the universe.'

Accompanying this description, with which none of you will find fault, there is in the London edition of his work a beautiful copperplate engraving of the Falls,— which in beauty, to say the least, is equal to many engravings of the same that have been offered to the public within the last ten years. At the time of his visit, the island below the Falls was full of eagles' nests, the rapids rendering them secure from the attacks of man or beast.

After a careful inspection of the Falls, he continued his journey to the point where his predecessor, Hennepin, stopped, to the River St. Francis. Carver believed that this country was destined to be settled ; he even partitioned the lands of Wisconsin and Eastern Minesota into subordinate colonies. These he divided by dotted lines and numbered, that future adventurers might readily, by referring to the map, choose a commodious

and advantageous situation.   Tract No. I, or Eastern
Minesota, is thus described :

'The country within these limits, from its situation,
is colder than any of the others, yet I am convinced
that the air is much more temperate than in those pro-
vinces that lie in the same degree of latitude to the east
of it.   The soil is excellent, and there is a great deal of
land that is free from woods in the parts adjoining to
the Mississippi, whilst on the contrary, the Northeastern
borders are well wooded.   Towards the heads of the
River St. Croix, rice grows in great plenty, and there is
abundance of copper.   Though the Falls of St. Anthony
are situated at the Southeast corner of this division, yet
that impediment will not totally obstruct the navigation.
As the River St. Croix, which runs through a great part
of the Southern side of it, enters the Mississippi just below the Falls, and flows with so gentle a current, that
it affords a convenient navigation for boats.   This tract
is about one hundred miles from N. W. to S. E., and
twenty from N. E. to S. W.'

Living more than a quarter of a century before Evans
and Fitch and Fulton made their incipient attempts to
apply steam to the propulsion of boats on the Delaware
and Hudson rivers, he could not conceive how vessels
could ascend with ease above the Forks of the Ohio ;

yet he looked for the time which we are destined to see, when by canals, or 'shorter cuts, a communication may be opened by water with New-York by way of the Lakes.'

On Carver's return from the Falls, he ascended the St. Peter's River, and wintered. Concerning his residence there, we can say but little, as many of his statements are incredible; especially that which says that he learned the Sioux, one of the most difficult of the Indian languages, in a few months, so that he could deliver speeches in that tongue.

Descending the St. Peter's in the spring, after attending a great council of the Sioux just below St. Paul, he proceeded with a deputation of their number by the way of the Chippewa River and Lake Superior to Mackinaw.

Returning to Great Britain, he communicated the information he obtained to several gentlemen of wealth and intelligence. In the year 1774, Richard Whitworth, a member of Parliament, a Colonel Rogers and Carver had determined to proceed to America and built a Fort at Lake Pepin, and then ascend the St. Peter's and Missouri Rivers, until they discovered the River Oregon, whose sources they supposed were on the other side of the ridge dividing the waters of the Gulf of Mexico from those of the Pacific Ocean. On that coast another post was to have been established, and from thence they expected to be able to reach the countries of Asia by some short passage. These plans, however, were all frustrated by the war between the American Colonies and the mother country. That Captain Carver made many statements not consistent with truth, cannot be denied ; yet no one can read his book without acknowledging that he was a man of vigorous intellect and keen observation. When we remember, that the European nations expected every traveller to tell some wondrous tale upon his return, and believed it more readily on account of its improbability ; that the age had not quite passed when ' feathers could be produced which had dropped from the tail of a phœnix ; that ostriches were to be seen which unlike the birds of the present day, had not pecked their way into the world through an egg shell, but had been born alive ; that bones were plentiful, of giants, with whom Goliath was a dwarf; that petrified babies were not rare ;' we ought not to be surprised that he describes a thunder storm in the vicinity of Mendota, 'so violent that the earth shook and the lightning flashed along the ground in streams of sulphur ;' nor that he should print a speech which he says he delivered in the Dakota language, after a residence of a few months among the Nation.

After the explorations of General, then Lieut. Pike, the United States Government in 1823 determined that 'an expedition be immediately fitted out for exploring the River St. Peter's, and the country situated on the Northern boundary of the United States between the Red River of Hudson's Bay and Lake Superior.' The commander of the expedition was Major Stephen Long. The party left Philadelphia and proceeded via Fort Dearborn (the site of the city of Chicago) to Prairie du Chien, where they arrived on the 19th of June. On the 2d of July, the party passed the narrowest place of the Mississippi, and landed for a few moments six miles below St. Paul, to examine a stone which was then held in high veneration among the Indians on account of the red pigment with which it was covered, hence now called Red Rock. ' It is a fragment of sien-ite, which is about four and a half feet in diameter. It is not surprising that the Indians should have viewed this rock with some curiosity, and deemed it wonderful, considering that its character differs so materially from the rocks which are found in that neighborhood. A man who lives in a country where the highest hills are wholly formed of sand-stone and secondary limestone, will necessarily be struck with the peculiar characters of the first specimen of the granite that comes under his notice, and it is not to be wondered at that one who " sees God in all things" should have made part of a stone an object of worship.'—(Long's Expedition.)

Above Red Rock, they visited the cemetery which had been mentioned by Carver more than a half century previous, and saw scaffolds supporting rude coffins.— At a little distance below St. Paul they passed the village of Kaposia, as before stated on the East side of the river, and called ' Petit Corbeau,' after the Chief who resided there. This tribe now live on the other side, and is the mission station of Dr. Williamson. The Indians that are so constantly in the streets of St. Paul, reside there. The cave discovered by Carver below St. Paul, the party of 1823 did not visit, but the little cave above that town, which we have inappropriately marked on our maps ' Carver's Cave,' a place which Carver never saw, and was never discovered until 1811.

On the night of the 2d July, Long and his party reached Fort Snelling, which work had been commenced about four years before.

On the 6th of July, members of this party walked to the Falls of St. Anthony, which they began to ford.— Some of the company, however, found great difficulty in stemming the current, and reached this side of the rapids much exhausted.

By Major Long's measurement, the perpendicular fall
of water was found to be about sixteen feet. A quarter
. of a century ago, the United States had two mills in
operation here, which were watched by a sergeant's
guard.

In the narrative of Major Long's expedition, we not
only find for the first time, the legend of Winona, who,
thwarted in marrying the object of her love, dashed herself to pieces from the lofty bluff on Lake Pepin, which
will always be called Maiden's Rock, but he also gives
the following legend of the Falls, which he learned
from an Indian :

'An Indian of the Dakota or Sioux Nation, had
united himself early in life to a youthful female, whose
name was Ampato Sapa. With her he lived happily
for several years. Two interesting children gathered
around their lodge fire, from day to day, and they loved
to think that they were "their little ones." The man
was skilled as a hunter, and drew around him many
families. Desirous of being more intimately connected
with him, some of them suggested that a man of his
skill ought to possess more than one wife, to wait upon
him and his friends. They assured him that if he
would increase the number of his wives, that he would
increase his influence, and soon be recognized as a Chief.

Ambition overcame his affection, and he secretly took a
second wife. Being desirous to introduce his new bride
to his lodge in a way that would not displease his first
love, he said to the mother of his children, " You know
that I can love no woman so fondly as I doat upon you ;
with regret have I seen you of late subjected to toils
which must be oppressive to you, and from which I
would gladly relieve you. I have therefore resolved
upon taking another wife, but she shall always be subject to your control, as she will always rank in my
affections second to you."

' With deep grief did his first wife listen to these
words. She pleaded all the endearments of their past
life ; she spoke of his former fondness for her, and bade
him beware of introducing another woman into the
lodge. Finding that he could not persuade her to be
contented, he informed her that he had already procured
another woman to share the lodge with her.

' Distressed at this information, she watched her opportunity, stole away from the cabin with her children,
and fled to a distance, where her father was. With
him she remained until a party of Indians went up the
river to hunt. In the spring, as they returned with
their furs, they encamped near these Falls. In the
morning the band left, but she lingered near the spot.

Having launched her light canoe, she entered with her children. Paddling down the rapids, she began to sing her death song.

'Her friends saw the movement, but they were too late to prevent. Her voice grew less and less distinct as she approached the edge of the Falls. For a moment, the canoe paused at the brink, enveloped with spray, then with a sudden plunge it darted down, carrying all of its contents to instant death.

'The Indians believe that in the morning a voice is heard, singing a doleful ditty along the edge of the Fall, and that it ever dwells upon the inconstancy of her husband. Some even assert that her spirit has been seen wandering near the spot, with her children wrapped to her bosom.'

We have thus given you a brief review of the principal French, English, and American travels to this widely celebrated spot.

A few months has worked great changes in the vicinity of these 'roaring waters.'

Less than two years ago, a divine of European as well as American reputation, visited this place, and felt that he was in a far distant land. Were he to repeat his visit, on every seventh day, though he might not hear the doleful ditty of Ampato Sapa, he would listen to the songs ' of a Saviour's dying love,' mingling with the majestic chorus of ' many waters ;' he would witness to-night, an audience not less intelligent than those gathered on similar occasions, ' in the smiling villages of the East ;' and a library, as yet small, in which however the last new novel is not conspicuous, but the works of Burke, Carlyle's and Headley's Cromwell, Arnold's History of Rome, and the Essays of Talfourd, Stephens and Channing.

Though the citizens of the most Northern village in the Valley of the Mississippi, you show to the world that extremes are often in close proximity ; that· the dwellers on the borders of an Indian country can commune with the noblest and best of minds, through their works, and appreciate, as well as any in the world, the voice of a living ministry, and the truths of the Sacred Writings."

CHAPTER XVII.

BEING desirous of doing all that I can towards bet-
tering the condition of my brethren, I here subjoin four
letters, originally addressed to the "Saturday Evening
Post" of Philadelphia, on the subject of Indian Civilization,—the plan which I have presented before different
Legislatures, and recently in a Memorial presented in
both Houses of Congress for their action.

I am happy to say that there is a universal approval
of this plan throughout the Union ; and it is my design
to request the General Government of this country that
they may sooner or later take these Indians under their
care, and have the credit of dealing justly with her long
abused red races. If Congress does not do any thing
in the present first session of the thirty-first Congress,
I shall go again—and just as often as they meet I shall
press this subject before them, until something is done.
The remarks here penned may be also applied in the

case of our Nation, who are now becoming demoralized yearly by alcoholic drinks.

I desire the reasons here given to be weighed by all impartial readers, and if any lack of soundness in our arguments be found, let it not be laid to the weakness of the cause we advocate, but to the writer's deficiency for such a work.

INDIAN CIVILIZATION.

MR. EDITOR.—Your readers will have noticed by the papers throughout the Union, the plan I have presented before the American public of my endeavors to save a remnant of the scattered Indian tribes of the Northwest.

I will endeavor to give a short outline, in three or four letters, of the matter as follows:

1. Why the Indians have not improved, and why they have decreased in numbers when coming in contact with the Europeans, since the first commencement of their intercourse until the present.

2. The fears I entertain that they never will hold a peaceable possession of any great portion of the West.

3. The plan I advocate, and its practicability.

4. The benefit it must be to the American Government, and to the Indians.

I. In this letter : *Why they have not improved, and why they have decreased in numbers.*

To give a statement of all the disadvantages they have had to encounter would not be in accordance with my present object, nor with the necessity imposed on me with reference to your columns ; yet I will mention a few. In their intercourse with the frontier settlers they meet the worst classes of pale faces. They soon adopt their foolish ways and their vices, and their minds being thus poisoned and preoccupied, the morality and education which the better classes would teach them are forestalled. This is not to be wondered at when it is generally known that the frontier settlers are made up of wild, adventurous spirits, willing to raise themselves by the downfall of the Indian race. These are traders, spirit-sellers, horse thieves, counterfeiters and scape-gallowses, who neither fear God nor regard the laws of man. When the Indians come in contact with such men, as representatives of the American people, what else could be expected of them ? It is not strange, that, seeing as he does the gross immorality of the whites whom he meets, and the struggle between the pale face for wrong and the red man for right, which begins when they first meet, and ends not until one dies, that he refuses to follow the footsteps of the white man in the

attainment of science. The majority having never been
in the society of the good, religious and refined, they
know but little of the advantages of civilization.

There has been another class of men who have kept
pace with the frontier, whose fathers and friends were
killed in the wars in the more Easterly States some
years ago by the Indians ; these having such implaca-
ble hatred against the poor Indians, do all they can to
enrage one race against the other, and if possible involve
the two in war, that they may engage in their favorite
work of depredation.

II. *Their love of Adventurous Life.*

Their fathers having been Nimrods, in a literal sense,
they have followed in their footsteps.

Not that I would have you suppose that there is no
such thing as teaching the American Indian the peaceful arts of agriculture, for he has already proved himself
teachable. The suddenness with which the American
people have come upon them, has prevented them from
gradually acquiring the arts of civilized life ; and leaving local employment, they have hunted for a living,
and thus perpetuated that independent, roaming disposition which was their early education.

III. *The agitation of mind they experience* in the belief that Government will want their lands and they be
removed to the West.

None but an Indian can, perhaps, rightly judge of the deleterious influence which the repeated removals of the Indians has wrought, since they began in the days of Jefferson, and have been continued by succeeding administrations, until now. Fear has prevented the Indian from making any very great advancement in agricultural science.

Having seen the removal of other Indian tribes, they have been conscious of the fact that the Government may and doubtless will want more land, and they be obliged to sell at whatever price Government may see fit to give, and thus all improvements they might have made would become useless to them.

In some instances, the Missionaries have done well in subduing the wild and warring dispositions of the Indians, but these lessons have been lost by the removal of the Indians Westward, and should he say aught, he is represented by the agents in an antagonistical attitude towards his own Government, *and the Indian has been the sufferer.*

IV. *The want of Schools of the character that are required for the Education of the Indians.*

I mean schools where the whip may be dispensed with as the motive power of acquiring education, and where rational beings are to be taught in a rational

P

manner. This whipping to learn is brutish and degrading—I might add, savage.

Gentle persuasion is that *cord* which has done the most for me and others. Many a school-teacher who has gone into the Indian country, had just as much right to become a teacher *to the Indians*, as I have to sit in the place of "Old Rough and Ready."

You will tell me, no doubt, that the Indians have been taught the advantages of education—that some even have gone and attended, not only the common school, but schools of a high order, colleges, and have returned to the forest again—have put on the blanket and roamed the woods. This has not always been the case. I might name a great many, who, to my knowledge, have done and are now doing well for themselves and for their people.

The reasons for their returning back again, were the absence of a good moral training, and their not having learned any trade with which to be employed on their leaving the schools. Having no employment, and no income, they found themselves in possession of all the qualities of a gentleman, without the requisite funds to support themselves.

Some of their teachers where they went, knowing only Christianity in theory, and not by a practical knowledge of the persuasive influences of its truths in the mind and soul, how could they teach them what they are destitute themselves? Open the pages of inspiration—and as fast as the clouds of ignorance shall roll away, let the warm rays from Him who smiles from the sky, into the soul. The mind of the Indian, well polished, shall then shine like the pure pearl from the deep. The cause of Education and Christianity must be to him what the wings are to eagles, *both must be exercised* before he can arise aloft.

Teaching the Indians in their own language what little some have learned, is one of those errors in which the majority of Missionaries have fallen, unintentionally, all over the country. I have endeavored to persuade them to teach our people English, and their course afterwards tells me— *We know better than you do*—and, therefore, a great amount of time, and a tremendous amount of money has been expended in translating and publishing a few books. We have been able to read these, but not one sentence of English. Our language perpetuates our own ideas of civilization, as well as the old usages in our Nation; and, consequently, how limited our field of acquiring knowledge! On the other hand, by giving them an English education, you introduce them into the endless field of English literature, and from the accumulated experience of the past, they might learn the elements which would produce the greatest amount of good to our Nation. The English language, it is true, is very hard to learn, but since it is to be the universal language in all lands, the sooner you give them this the better. I conclude this part of my letter by stating that the most requisite things for the Indian are these three—a mechanical or an agricultural education, a high-toned literature, and a rational moral training. Give him these—you make him exalted.— Deprive him of these—you make him degraded.

V. *The great quantity of Land which they have reserved to themselves for the purpose of hunting.*

This wild field, filled with a variety of game, perpetuates their natural propensity of living by the use of the bow and arrow; instead of following the plough and having the hoe in hand. When they can* have a piece of land they can call their own, and so limited that the scarcity of game will oblige them to till the soil for a subsistence, then they will improve, and the sooner this state of things is brought about will be the better.

VI. *The mode generally adopted by the Missionaries in introducing Christianity among the Indian Tribes.*

I know I shall be censured here—I can only appeal to the experience of the past, and leave every one to decide for himself. The Indian, not knowing abstract truths, cannot possibly understand the foundation of the many doctrinal views which he is desired to learn and adopt. Forms of worship, varied as they are, have been urged on him, and in being perplexed, his mind thus is prejudiced to Christianity.

Veneration and devotion make up the Indian's heart. Take him as he is, and lead him, and he will soon see the right from the wrong. We want also educated men. It has been the idea of some that any thing will do for the Indians.

Other reasons might be given, did space allow ; now, I proceed to give, in conclusion, a few of the reasons why their numbers have been lessened.

1. *The Diseases introduced by Europeans.*

The Indian Nations had no small pox or measles.— The small pox has destroyed thousands since it has been introduced into this country. Entire families have perished. Many an ill-fated tribe have followed their ancestors down to the grave, haggard, diseased, wretched and loathsome, by the disease which keeps pace with the debauchery towards the West.

These diseases, not many of them being known be fore, they knew not how to check their disastrous pro gress.

2. *Wars which they have made on each other since
the introduction of fire-arms.*

Before this, the weapons they used against one another were not so disastrous as the rifle has been since.
With the gun they have been as expert as they were
with the bow and arrow. Champlain, in the year 1609,
supplied the Algonquins of the North with the weapons
of war, that they might successfully wage war with the
Six Nations. The Dutch supplied the Six Nations
with the same materials. The Spaniards of the
South and others, might be cited, which history relates.
They receiving those weapons of war from a civilized and Christianized nation, guaranteed a free use of
them.

3. *Wars which have raged in this country between the
whites.*

During these wars the Indian has been called from
the woods to show his fearless nature, and for obeying,
and showing himself fearless, it is said of him that he is
"a man without a tear." He has been stigmatized
with the name—"a savage,"—by the very people who
called for his aid, and he gave it. In the midst of these
mighty contests, the Indian has been put in the front
ranks, in the most dangerous positions, and has consequently been the greatest loser.

4. *And lastly— The introduction of spirituous liquors.*
This has been greater than all other evils combined.
Intemperance and disease. The fire-water has done its
work of disaster. By it the glad shouts of the youth of
our land has died away in wails of grief! Fathers have
followed their children to their graves. Children have
sent their wail of woe, echoing from vale to vale. And
around the cheering fires of the Indian, the white man
has received the gain of avarice. Peace and happiness
entwined around the fire-side of the Indian once. Union,
harmony, and a common brotherhood cemented them all.
But as soon as these vile drinks were introduced, dissipation commenced, and the ruin and downfall of a noble
race has gone on—every year lessening their numbers.
Wave after wave of destruction has gone on—the raven-
wings of the angel of death have covered their fires, and
still unsatisfied, it screams for more victims—all, all,—
yes, all for "*model New England rum.*" The ministry
of this country, and the sluggards in the cause of humanity, say now : *There is a fate or certain doom on*
the Indians, therefore we need do nothing for them.
How blasphemous! First you give us rum by the thousand barrels, and, before the presence of God and this
enlightened world, point to God, and charge him as the
murderer of the unfortunate Indians.

"Oh, Mercy, oh, Mercy! look down from above,
Great Creator, on us Thy sad children with love."

Yes, save us from such orthodoxy! The laws of na
ture deranged in the Indian, both morally and physically,
has been the consequence of his sinking condition.

I have already taken too much of your space. I must
conclude. My next will be the fears I entertain they
will not hold their lands to any great extent this side of
the Rocky Mountains.

Excuse all errors, for I have by a railroad accident
been thrown on my bed.

Am, sir, yours, in the cause of humanity.

K.

————

INDIAN CIVILIZATION.—NO. II.

MR. EDITOR,—In this letter I will give you the
grounds of my fears why the Indians will never have a
permanent hold upon any part of the Western country,
unless by special act of Congress.

1. *Their position upon the press of emigration.*—
In this way for years the fires of the Indian lodge have
been removed West. Their rights have been trampled
upon by the settlers, and this, with other annoyances,
have ever unsettled the minds of the Indians—the con

sequence has been, and will be, that they will remove, step by step, to escape this annoyance.

The present belief of the Western and South-western Indians, that they never will be again moved, and that the land that they now occupy is to be their own forever—what sort of a guarantee do they have of their continuing on their lands unmolested? Will not the same plea which was given to remove the New-York, Massachusetts, Ohio and Georgia Indians—will not the same plea of necessity (and, as some say, an act of kindness to them) be urged on those on the other side of the Father of Waters as has been urged this side? If not this, enterprise—yes, Yankee enterprise, will require railroads to be laid out, canals to be opened, military roads cut through the land of the Indians in the West, and their land must either be bought from them or taken. And when this is done, or commenced to be done, they will cease to work their lands, since such labor would not be for their benefit, but for those who must occupy it when they leave it. The delightful fields of the Indians in Georgia were the great objects which the white men desired.

2. *The quantity of land* they have reserved to themselves, has retarded their progress in the acquirement of agricultural science. They have lived on the game

which roamed in their woods, which has called off their attention from the soil. They will still neglect the cultivation of the soil, since it is easier to hunt for game for a living than to toil in the field. This quantity is a detriment to us—we do not want so much land. But, what we have, give it to us forever.

3. *The quality is another.* There is a rich spot of land this side of the desert below the Rocky Mountains, the only rich land, and the Indian has been placed on this like a barrier. The land so occupied, *if not culti-vated,* the pale face will reason himself into the idea that the Great Spirit intended to make the whole of North America a farm yard, and thereby justify himself for taking to till what the Indian could not improve.

4. *Necessity will oblige him to sell.* They have, within my knowledge, reasoned this way. Our fathers sold their lands to the Government, and lived on the proceeds of the sale, and soon the Government will want to buy *this land,* and our children will live on the annui-ties as we now do on ours. So, they will fare no worse than we have. In this way they become impoverished, and they to sustain soul and body a few years of linger-ing misery, must sell their land piece by piece, until all is gone and they must suffer.

Much greater and certain evils are yet to be appre-
hended, arising from another source, which is this :

5. *The scarcity of game for food*, must cause suffering among the Indians, and a world of trouble to the
frontier settlers. Where will the Indian go to get any
thing to feed his children, but to the frontier for the cattle of the settlers for food? and this will cause war and
bloodshed.

The game is being killed more and more every year.
It is computed by recent travellers in the buffalo country, that this game alone is killed at the rate of one
hundred thousand every year, by trappers and the In
dians, for their hide and tongues, which are sold t(
traders on the Upper Missouri. Game of all kinds is
disappearing this side of the Rocky Mountains. Twelve
years ago we could go seventy-five miles West of Dubu-
que, Iowa, on the Mississippi, for game of every kind up
to buffalo ; now, I travelled last summer four hundred
miles West of the above mountains towards the Missouri
River, and found no game of any kind ! When, by
force of circumstances, the Indian is obliged to live on
the cattle of the frontiers—as soon as the first bullock is
killed, the cry will be heard, " The Indians are coming
on us." The answer will be, " To arms, to arms," and
the soldiery of the United States must be sent to go and

destroy a few dying and gasping Indians. The boom of the cannon and the rattle and peal of the drum will sing the dirge of the once free and powerful sons of America. Desperation will drive the Indian to die at the cannon's mouth—for it is then he will think of the land of his forefathers, which will nerve him to the field of war !—mustering his armies on the peaks of the cliffs of the West, they will shout to each other. On one hand, far off below, the dying fires of his race lie scattered, and the graves of his ancestors desecratad—his children scattered where he has been driven. On the other hand he will see the races of the Pacific driven to the Eastward from the Valley of the Columbia. It is there I expect to see what our forefathers have not yet witnessed. My blood runs cold when I think of it.— Great God, save us from realizing the horrors of an exterminating war !

6. *Their isolated condition in detached numbers*, will be the means of preventing the acquirement of knowledge. When there is no stimulus to improve, there will be no idea of learning much. In small bodies, they retain all the feelings of their forefathers, and will continue this way. The American Government has addressed us like different Nations, instead of addressing us as an Indian Nation, and as one family; they have in this

way perpetuated our differences towards each other.—
The same law which governs the masses of people
of all nations (civilized) among the pale faces, in some
degree would then keep them at peace with each other.
The law of necessity—the law of a common interest—
the law of love, are so many influences which ought to
have operated on them before ; since, then, these are
wanting, the feuds which have been kept up must
necessarily exist for some time. The tribes, being
weakened by their hostilities, can never prosper. But
collect them in a large body by themselves, and commence rationally to adopt a system of pupilage which
will be well adapted for the young ; and one good man
would be like a light-house in a storm, who would warn
and guide the rest.

In my next I will give the plan of concentrating the
Northwest Indian tribes and its practicability.

I am, sir, yours, in the cause of humanity,

K.

MR. EDITOR :—In my last, I gave you some reasons why I think the possessions of the Indians are still precarious. In this, I propose to give an *outline of the project of civilizing the Northwestern Tribes and its practicability.*

My plan is to get a grant of land from the Congress of the United States, about one hundred and fifty miles square, as a perpetual reserve for all the Northwest Tribes this side of the Rocky Mountains—where the half-civilized on the frontiers might live permanently to enjoy the fruits of their labor, and immediately form a government of their own, from the crude state in which they are, and gradually introduce the most simple laws to govern them, as they may need.

1. A Governor to be appointed by the President of the United States, to be a white man, and the Lieutenant-Governor to be an Indian.

2. A Secretary, to be a white man, or an Indian, if any is found capable to fill the office, who shall transmit all the laws of the Indian territory to the Congress of the United States every year.

3. That the Governor and Lieutenant-Governor shall convene all the Indian tribes within the said territory,

that they may organize such form of Government as
may be for their interest. The Chiefs of each tribe to
become the delegates from their number, and this to be
every three years.

4. That all white people who travel through this reserved land, must travel with a special license from the
Agent of the American Government who may reside
here. And, that all the white people who may reside
as Government officers, missionaries and school teachers,
must reside by such license, to be issued once a year ;
and all who have no license, must be looked upon as
intruders.

5. That a court of law be instituted, composed half
of white people and half of Indians, who shall decide
all grievances between the two races, the Indian and
the pale face, instead of harassing the Government
with them.

6. That the gathering of the Indians be voluntary on
their part, and by giving them inducements, they need not
be compelled by arbitrary means to leave their own lands.

7. That a military post be placed near the centre of
the Indian Territory, and manned, to give security to
individuals who may travel or reside there ; but more
to keep off the *white savages*, who deal in fire water.

8. That the Indian Government be represented in

Washington by a Commissioner, to be appointed by the
General Council of the Indian Confederacy in the mean-
time, until the state of intelligence among them should
require a more intimate connection with the Federal
States—then, if deemed proper, to form one of the States
of the Union.

9. Schools to be supported by a general fund, which
will accumulate as they cede their present lands to the
Government, and those schools to be connected with the
education of the plough, and the tillage of the soil.

Next of importance is the *location.* The place I have
named is the unsettled land known as the West of Minesota, next to the banks of the Missouri. The great Sioux
River, from its junction to its source, to become the Eastern boundary—from the source of the Sioux River, draw
a line Westward to the Missouri River, to become the
Northern boundary. Next, the channel of the Missouri
River to the place of beginning, would constitute a territory large enough for all such purposes.

The reasons why I have named this as being the
most suitable for them are the following :

1. The *great national* highways, which will soon be
opened by the demands of enterprize of the West, must
be South of this, and thereby would not come in contact
with the Indian population.

2. The *climate* is most suitable for their natures.

3. It would also be favorable to them in a commercial point of view, between the two greatest valleys and river, the Missouri and the Mississippi.

4. The *distance* West would be far enough to cause the removal of all the various Indian tribes to be gradual.

5. The *central location* of this country would be favorable for the removal of the different tribes from the surrounding country of 500 or 600 miles.

The question naturally rises in the minds of all who may have studied the interest of the Indians, *whether such a scheme is practicable.* I think it is.

1. The *interest* of the Indians being in the hands of the American Government, that interest could be used for the promotion of the good of the Indians, and by an annual distribution of the annuities of the Indians in the central portion of the territory, would attach them to their homes and country.

2. The *treaties* which are to be made, would so far become easy for them to be moving on this territory, and as the Indians are to be removed any how, why should it be more unpalatable to the Government to re-move them to this tract, as they have always made out to move the Indians West whenever they have needed their lands ?

3. The *social* character of the Indians. They would rather live in towns, or near each other, particularly when they are civilized. The oftener they could see one another, the more rapidly their jealousies would cease to exist. Their children, growing up together, would soon acquire a mutual attachment and regard for each other's welfare.

4. The *languages* of the Northwest tribes are so far similar, that they soon would learn to understand one another. The Ojibway language, or the Algonquin dialect, is spreading all over the country of the Northwest. The traditional stories which are related by our forefathers, indicate that our common stock was one.— And to reunite the scattered families, and preserve the few, would soon become an object in their minds.

5. By giving encouragement to those who would go there to settle, there would be no difficulty in getting them there, for the educated portion of them would be the first who would settle in that country; and they are the ones I would encourage, for they would be the ones who would form such a Government as would best suit the Indian's wants and condition.

6. By a proclamation of the President of the United States, calling upon all the Northwest Indian tribes, and telling them that a *home*, a permanent home is provided,

they soon would obey it, and go, if not in collective bodies, at least individually.

7. *War must then cease to exist.* There will be no game, nor any territory to fight for. They soon must learn, that in destroying *one* it is to strike a blow at *all,* and the public opinion will triumph, and frown down any such acts of misdemeanor of the inhabitants.

8. Gradually the Chiefship, which is hereditary, would cease to exist, for this is one of the greatest barriers to their civilization. By giving the rule and authority to the well educated, their improvement would be rapid ; but, heretofore, the elder Indians have ruled, and their prejudicial views of education, have ever unfitted them to become a fit medium of instruction to their people. And in this way many will then study hard to fit themselves to become the rulers of the Nation.

9. The *comparatively peaceable* condition of the Northwest Indian tribes at present is favorable. The wars which raged in years past, are not now in existence.— The spirit of war is dying away at the approach of civilization Westward, and the more peaceable acts of civilized life are being practiced by them.

10. The *great number of young men* that are among the various Indian tribes, who are ready to carry forward any benevolent measure which may be supported

by the Government of the United States. The New-York Indians are now so far civilized as to have a Republican Government of their own. There are young men in that Nation who would do honor to any position in the arrangement of a Government for the Indians.—The Chippeway Nation has a great number of well educated young men. The Stockbridges, Oneidas and Shawnees, all these have been blessed with a partial civilization.

Many other reasons might be given besides the above. I will close now, and in my next I will speak of the benefits which must accrue to the *American Government* and to the *Indians*.

I am, sir, yours, in the cause of humanity,

K.

INDIAN CIVILIZATION.—NO. IV.

Mr. Editor:—Having stated the reasons why I deem my scheme practicable, I will, in conclusion, allude to the advantages that would accrue, not only to the United States, but to the Indians.

To the American Government.

1. This system would simplify the Indian department.

2. They would not have so much perplexity in ad justing difficulties.

3. The outlay in Indian agencies would be lessened.

4. Establish a court of justice in the Indian territory, and no trouble would be had with them, as the difficulties would be legally settled. For sometimes it has been the hasty means used to suppress the encroachments of the Indian on the white man which have caused the disgraceful wars which this country has seen. Such would be obviated.

5. The expense of fortifying the Western country from the encroachments of the Indians would be dispensed with, and even now they are not actually required. But if the government *must* build forts, and establish military posts, let there be one, in the center of the new Indian territory, to give efficiency to the laws of the Indian government, to protect the peace and persons in that country.

Go in the spirit of the illustrious William Penn, that noble personification of Christianity, and you will have no trouble with the Indians this side of the Rocky Mountains.

6. The outlay for transporting the Indians would cease to be a burden. I believe the Indians would now go of their own accord, did they know that the land could be thus occupied by them.

7. The buying of the land from the Indians over and over would not then have to be done.

8. The peaceful and friendly relations that must then exist would be one of the strongest bonds of union in time of peace, and cause them to be neutral in time of war.

9. Besides the above considerations, there are higher motives which ought to prompt the members of Congress—motives arising in the consideration that they are only forwarding the great design of Heaven, to improve the races of this country. By intelligence enlarge the arena of human freedom, and your leading the Indian may be like the noble eagle's first flight with its young to the sun.

The advantages to the Indians.

1. By having *permanent* homes, they would soon enjoy the fruit of their labor. Poverty would be unknown, plenty would reign, and cheerfulness aid them in their work.

2. Seminaries of learning would be permanently located ; every stone you laid for the foundation of a school would tell. The repeated removals of the Indians have retarded the progress of moral and physical training among them, and caused many good men to become discouraged in their alms-giving for their improvement

It has not been so much the fault of the Indian as it has been the error of judgment in the distribution of these means.

3. The appropriation by the United States, for the education of the Indians, of $10,000, would then be a benefit to those for whom it is intended. Let the Government endow a college in the central part of the Indian country, and it would have an influence for good to the end of time.

4. And besides this, what an amount would accumulate, were all the school funds which the Indians have even now, given by the Government in its generosity for their annuities, and which now many Indian tribes know not what to do with, thus appropriated. Concentration of means and of effort on the part of the benevolently-disposed, must necessarily, in the process of time, do a great deal of good.

5. In treaties which are to be made, if a policy could be pursued in such a way as to get the annuities of the Indians to be paid in part toward the national education of the whole colony, much of what is needed in reference to means would be so augmented as to give whole districts of country the benefit of an enlightened education.

But, say you, How will you reconcile the different denominations of Christians who may go there to teach?

Having no predilection to *division* and discord, I would
not have one dollar of the money which the generosity
of the Government should give, go toward perpetuating
discordant elements. No ! I want to make the great
family of the Indians ONE, should I live long enough—
one in interest, *one* in feeling, *one* while they live, and
one in a better world after death.

6. Emulation among themselves would spring up;
and each would labor for the others' good—a spirit of
rivalry would soon be seen were a premium to be given
to those who should raise the largest amount of agricultural produce.

7. The result of all this would be a rapid increase of
intelligence among the Indians, and steps would soon
be taken to have a representation in Congress.

It is hoped that, without making any special plea for
the red men, that sense of justice which dwells in the
heart of every *true American* will lead the members of
Congress to give the above reasons a passing consideration.

KAH-GE-GA-GAH-BOWH.

www.ingramcontent.com/pod-product-compliance
Lightning Source LLC
Chambersburg PA
CBHW030351270326
41926CB00009B/1056